The Alien Handbook:
A Guide to Extraterrestrials

Patrick De Haan CPCU

For permission, serialization, condensation, adaptions, or for our catalog of other publications, write to Ozark Mountain Publishing, Inc., P.O. box 754, Huntsville, AR 72740, ATTN: Permissions Department.

Library of Congress Cataloging-in-Publication Data

De Haan, Patrick – 1960 -

The Alien Handbook by Patrick De Haan

This book is about the connection to aliens/extraterrestrials through the means of channeling and their messages for us.

1. Aliens   2. Extraterrestrials   3. Channeling   4. Guardian Angels

I. Patrick De Haan, 1960- II. Extraterrestrials III. Channeling IV. Title

Library of Congress Catalog Card Number: 2017964431
ISBN: 9781940265483

Cover Art and Layout: www.vril8.com
Book set in: Times New Roman, Maiandra GD
Book Design: Tab Pillar
Published by:

OZARK
MOUNTAIN
PUBLISHING

PO Box 754, Huntsville, AR 72740
800-935-0045 or 479-738-2348; fax 479-738-2448
WWW.OZARKMT.COM
Printed in the United States of America

The Alien Handbook:
A Guide to Extraterrestrials

ex·tra·ter·res·tri·al

adjective
of or from outside the earth or its atmosphere
"searches for extraterrestrial intelligence"

noun
a hypothetical or fictional being from outer space, especially an intelligent one

The adjective definition is correct, but for the noun it is wrong. Living beings from "outer space" are not hypothetical or fictional.

Contents

Preface

REASONS NOT TO READ THIS BOOK

This first part of the preface is short and easy to write; you should not read this book if you believe aliens, extraterrestrials, and unidentified flying objects are one and all, a huge pile of fantasies. You might think the notion there are visitors to Earth from outer space is nothing more than a collection of fact-free theories offered up by people with far too much unproductive time on their hands, who choose to fill it with meaningless gibberish.

If any part of the foregoing rings true, this book could waste your time. *Atlas Shrugged* by Ayn Rand, *Catcher in the Rye* by J. D. Salinger, *Breakfast at Tiffany's* by Truman Capote, and almost anything by authors John Updike and Earnest Hemingway offer excellent returns on your reading time, an investment you likely often make if you've come this far. If this "trigger warning," a recent college student fad, saves you time and expense, you're welcome; I'm happy to do my part. Consider it a valuable detour along Literature Boulevard.

REASONS TO READ THIS BOOK

If on the other hand, you'd like to know more ...

The general absence of popularly accepted evidence regarding extraterrestrials (ETs) suggests there are none. Cold logic, however, says the absence of information neither confirms nor denies anything. Some evidence is simply a suggestion; the now-missing car parked outside last night "suggests" it was taken. Was it parked elsewhere but forgotten? Film at 6.

Chatter about ETs among humans is frequent. UFO sightings are well documented and often photographed. They are that "missing vehicle" about which little is known regarding ETs, beyond vague, "unconfirmed" witness statements and fuzzy photographs or videos.

As this book is completed, Earth enters a crucial phase for the development of the current civilizations. Life will be fundamentally transformed in ways most of us would deem unimaginable at the moment. There will be little imagination required as each phase unfolds but for the majority of mankind, each step will have to occur to be believed. A crucial, integral part of the changes will be the revelation that extraterrestrial visitors both exist and visit Earth regularly.

As the information becomes unmistakable, it will be easy to react along with the masses as the search for knowledge erupts and confusion likely rises also. Fear will be part of the mix and if allowed to overwhelm too many observers, will risk undermining the purpose ET visitors have for contact with humans and for revelation of their presence.

If you would like advance knowledge, you now have your reason to read this book.

Introduction

I don't remember when channeling started for me. I knew it was happening but I didn't know to call it that; in fact, I didn't even know what channeling was, growing up in the 1960s and '70s.

Awareness of eating and breathing don't require the study of anatomy. Most of us take those functions for granted, unless we're nurses or doctors. I went with the mind's flow, what seemed normal and typical for most people, simply because it always was and has been for me.

For most of my life, I took my thoughts for granted, just like food or air. I assumed my mind works the same way the mind does for almost everyone. I discovered gradually and steadily, that's not the case. Several things came together randomly and simultaneously, or so they seemed to.

The first hint was a hardcover book I randomly found, getting on a train in the mid-1990s. The book was brand new, as if fresh off a table of "New Releases" at a bookstore, no receipt or store bag, sticking out of a seatback pocket high enough to be easily seen. The passenger car of the train was empty except for me, and it had just started moving; obviously the owner had forgotten it and would be impossible to find. The book groaned and cracked when I opened it, the way brand-new, unopened hardcovers sometimes do. How did this one book make it this far, its cover never pulled apart?

Naturally I read it, and a certain part jumped out at me, describing what set me on a continuing journey of channeling, something that took years to understand.

I studied business administration way back when and got a job in commercial insurance. It became a career that took me around the world; one of my children was born overseas because of it. Over more than three decades, I often encountered interesting situations where channeled information really helped but sometimes hindered me. Not understanding where certain information came from, I nevertheless offered it up in good faith, only to discover that while most people appreciate information, candor, and insight, a small minority prefer others who remain in place and role, inside the comfort zone that small minority highly prefers for itself and everyone it meets. I sometimes got annoyed glances which all but asked, "How do you know what took me X years to get?" or worse, "How can you know what I don't know and be so accurate about what's coming? How?" I even got fired along the way a few times, despite making boatloads of profit for employers. I learned terrific life lessons; if not wrapped a certain way, good results sometimes aren't. I was a foreign-language teacher; more teaching of communication. My life's plan unfolds as designed.

My next big hint was a book I "encountered randomly" in a bookstore, written by a prominent local medium, who lived a dozen US states away at that time. It described channeling and how to do it. I couldn't seem to "get it" when I followed the book's advice, soon discovering I was already "getting it" and had been for decades. There was not much to learn, simply recognize what was already happening and begin separating incoming from self-generated material. A few years later I moved to the same town as that author psychic, and even though I've never met her even until today, I now understand my guardian angel guides were both telling me where I had already planned to live and what I'd eventually pursue, when we planned this lifetime together, by "giving" me that book.

My wonderful experiences in business, and the less-than-ideal reactions sometimes encountered, came into better focus.

Now keenly interested in the subject, I began looking for books on anything related to channeling; guardian angels, spirits, souls, Heaven. The information all flowed as easily and frustratingly as doing times tables from elementary school math, and I confess feeling constrained, wanting more.

One day I entered a mall bookstore, but was unable to find the "New Age" section. A young, dark-haired man calmly approached and asked what was I looking for. I told him and he gave me the aisle and directions without pointing or even looking toward where I should go. When I got to the register, I asked the cashier if she could find that clerk so I could thank him. She asked what he looked like; when I described him, she told me nobody even close to that description worked there.

Another day soon after, I was walking around looking for a mailbox and knew there had to be one nearby. Rather than accept information that came when it seemed to decide for itself, I tried to "activate" its arrival. I "quieted" my mind the way one book suggested, and listened for the answer. The "reply" thought popped into my head just like a million others had, except when I looked where the "thought" told me to go, voilà: mailbox! Now I could both receive AND request information.

I decided to ask my guardian angel (or angels) to appear physically, the way another book said is possible. While I was exercising, I asked for it to happen. Twenty minutes into a half-hour run, a gray-haired man in a dark overcoat and gray scarf appeared in the park, walking toward me. He calmly looked at me as I ran past, and gave me a gentle, confident smile. The sensation that he knew me very well overflowed, and even in that five-second encounter, I immediately sensed it was a person of trust and confidence. A few steps later it hit me that the "sighting" I'd asked for had just happened! I stopped short and turned around; there was no sign of him. I ran back and looked everywhere he could have gone. I even looked up into the trees; he disappeared just like the bookstore clerk. I realized I'd seen another of my angel guardian guides.

Around this time, my wife, kids, and I moved halfway across the USA, and I settled in after fifteen years of globetrotting. I didn't pursue channeling much. This dry period lasted for about a decade as my wife of now thirty years and I continued raising our kids and getting ready for the middle age we now solidly occupy.

Urges to write, abrupt career changes, and readings from outstanding mediums revealed to me why and how I had been getting information "out of thin air" the way I used to believe happened to everybody, a long time ago. Most importantly, it became obvious where things would lead if I followed. The itch was strong, and I scratched it.

Mediums or psychics do especially well when consulting another one, the way a doctor can often be a very good (*but sometimes bad*) patient. I received consistent feedback among four very talented psychics, all of whom told me writing and addressing of human society issues would be a strength and are a life purpose for me. I didn't have to think long about what had come through; the "names" of my guardian angels were offered, "names" I discovered I'd agreed with them to use, to help me both identify and describe them to others. I nicknamed my trio "The Committee" because of the way I get information which seems to come from a collective consciousness, rather than a single "person."

Have you ever seen a show or movie where two or more people speak simultaneously and say the exact same thing? Mostly this happens with singers and it's what usually happens when "The Committee" answers my questions, except I don't see, hear, or physically sense them. Nevertheless, information flows more clearly than listening to a lecture or watching a movie, better than most speech. I speak several languages and discovered that part of my life plan was to learn then apply translation and interpretation, to help put thoughts into human words. The bilingual or polyglots among readers know intrinsically what I mean.

Getting information from my guides is easier than listening to somebody speak then converting. Could I put channeled information into another language? ¡Claro que sí!

I scratched the itch and created a website. Reader questions and the incoming responses "from beyond" raised my awareness of telepathic, two-way communication with both souls of the "human dead"—*only our bodies pass away*—and mankind's visiting cousins from around the galaxy, ETs or extraterrestrial visitors. I then understood what had been happening most of my life, which I had simply and erroneously assumed was common. I asked questions and the answers made me feel like a veteran interviewer.

To date I've written enough channelings on a wide variety of subjects to outweigh *War and Peace* by Leo Tolstoy. The website receives a steady volume of hits and continues to grow, completely by word-of-mouth. I don't advertise it personally, except for a reader in Australia who offered to pay for a small "advert" in an Aussie monthly on the subject, which caused an immediate and sustained uptick in traffic.

Several hundred thousand website hits and a waterfall of questions and answers with readers, both about the channeled topics and other things, led to this book. I credit those reader questions; my previously low interest in ETs probably would not have gotten this book going.

I also discovered many inquisitors—not just inquirers—of and about channeled information, generally ask about the same topics: relationships (*family, friends, or romantic*), job and career, money, world events, and crime.

I've never been drawn to personal questions, and sometimes don't get much information. I avoid criminality for concern I'd be pursued by investigators (*or perpetrators*), but this point is moot. I simply don't get information about such things. I also discovered many people consulting a medium or psychic often come to the process with heavy preconceptions, and I expand on that aspect in chapter 2.

In mid-2015, my guides told me Donald Trump would become the next president of the USA. Relentlessly opposed by the competing political party and rejected by a good deal of his own, Trump nevertheless prevailed over more than twenty opponents from all sides, against all odds, sentiments, and predictions.

A reader asked me in April 2016 if Great Britain would vote to leave the European Union in the upcoming June referendum. My guides were unequivocal; Great Britain would vote to depart. Not being in the United Kingdom, I was not exposed to the media onslaught that showered the populace with polls, predictions, and analysis consistently saying the "Brexit" vote would confirm Great Britain's place in the EU. *Oooooops ...*

Come October 2016, another reader asked me about the USA's baseball championship, the World Series. It was historic because the Chicago Cubs had reached it for the first time in many decades and had not won in more than a century. My guides said, "Chicago in six," for the best-of-seven games series. Chicago won, but in seven games, the final one going right down to the wire. Even I started to doubt what I'd been given as I watched the last game. *Tsk tsk tsk ...*

So, what was it about that book I found on the train that motivated me? The author described moving to another city and being frustrated with finding a place to live. She was advised (by a faith healer I think—it's been twenty years since I read it) to imagine the perfect place; how it would look, what it should cost, where located, what type floors, wall colors, and so forth. She took that advice and dreamed. Soon after, she went to see another apartment in her ongoing search; it was exactly as she had imagined. As if her thoughts had created the place for her, or it already existed and her "imagination" was simply seeing something ready and waiting. Maybe a combination of both?

Those possibilities hooked me, and I have since been pursuing—and understanding much better—what time, Earth, and humanity involve, and the information supplied by my guardian angels and many other "spirit" entities we humans do not usually see with our eyes.

Channeling has become a common term, understood as tuning in to images and ideas, such as a celebrity's public image. Yes, it is, but it is much more, also; it's a two-way street of individual and mass communication for driving through oncoming, "incoming" traffic, where rules of the road go airborne.

In the case of this book, channeling reveals something that will likely fascinate, stun, amaze, and terrify a good deal of humankind. Off we go …

- 1 -
What Is an Extraterrestrial?

The word combines "terra" (Earth) and "extra" (beyond) to mean anything not a part of our planet. "Alien" is also a popular word but simply means foreign. Foreign means strange, unknown, or out of its normal, usual place.

Extraterrestrial visitors are more like humans than most animals on Earth, the majority of which are far more alien to human beings than the extraterrestrials.

Right about now, a few skeptics wavering between the two parts of the preface can hear their bullfeather detector going off and are reconsidering the decision to read this far. They—or you—are asking how the author knows this. The chapters that follow hold answers. This book isn't about the author or methods but also addresses them, along with and as the important parts, the ETs. There is no information about my life to improve yours. Readers will be interested in ET information, just as the book title says.

***

The similarity between human bodies and ETs exists because they are our cousins, for the most part. Many of them are bipeds, two-legged upright-walking creatures just as we are, and with two arms and a head that contains a brain. They have hands and feet and digits on them. They have skin and eyes and breathe air and digest nutrients.

The human story of Adam and Eve is a representation of a true event; the presence of humans on Earth is not an evolution of amoebas to fish to frogs to larger mammals to simians then humans. There are many natural species to Earth, and many have evolved just as science says they have. These animals and their predecessors have been evolving on Earth for many millions of years. Humans have been here for about fifty thousand.

We were created by extraterrestrial visitors who came to mine gold. The plan was not to create a new race of humanoid, but the visitors found the work tougher than expected and used their knowledge and ability to modify DNA to create a humanoid form. They simply used some of their own and crossed it with existing

1

animals they found here.

At about this point it is important to note that we are all spiritual beings with a soul that temporarily resides on Earth, in a body that carries our soul on a journey from birth and before, to death and passing. Then we return to our true home, what many of us refer to as Heaven.

The first humanoid beings were humanoid in the image of their creators, who were strongly admonished when their brethren back home on their planet of origin discovered what had been done to mine the gold. This specific ET civilization has not been back to visit beyond observing Earth.

What we call Neanderthal and Cro Magnon man were these first humanoids created by ET visitors. The general differences in what we believe were different stages of evolution were more like upgrades to the DNA, modifications made for the better adaptation of the new race to Earth. These improvements were made by the masters of the first miners, upon discovery of what had been done. Many of the skull and bone differences anthropologists have identified were natural variations between individual members of the race, just as occurs with humans. We're not all the same height, weight, and build, and neither were these first humanoids on Earth.

The mining stage was not long lived; after several decades of Earth time, by the counting of Earth rotations and revolutions to measure it, the mineral extraction was complete. ET visitor oversight and monitoring of Earth by this creator group continued for approximately three centuries after that. At this point, the adjustment and upgrades to human DNA were considered done and the new race self-sufficient and evolving naturally.

From this point until now, a noninterference prime directive was put in place. Several ET civilizations were aware of what had been done; these members of the already formed association or coalition of societies in this sector or quadrant of the galaxy have protected Earth against interference, incursions, or intervention by any visitors. Observation and inspection are allowed only and great care is taken to do nothing that would distort the course of human and Earth development beyond what natural forces and human choice produce.

Humans have developed in many unique ways; we vary widely in appearance and characteristic. The vast differences in race are latent DNA evolution caused by environmental factors that all humans carry in their genetic code. A group of Chinese would still evolve into an appearance similar to what is common in Scandinavia or Russia, if relocated to different climates for long enough. The complete change in human physical characteristics takes place over about fifty centuries, give or take.

The souls of the first humans to live on Earth joined the process in a similar way you joined the body, family, and place on Earth you have now. Willingly and with understanding of what would happen. Souls of humans are not solely human, in every incarnation or life experienced on Earth. It is possible and common to be a dog, horse, bear, or ant rather than a human being. The opportunity to experience a life on Earth will always find a willing taker. We all plan our lives and make a contract or agreement with ourselves to follow it, specific events written in. Free will remains in effect at all times, and the decisions we make to experience certain things can seem as if they are out of control. We design in this aspect of seemingly uncontrolled experiences, and we monitor ourselves as we go. Our souls choose guides and guardians to be with us each moment our bodies are on Earth, a great honor bestowed upon those chosen to accompany us.

The creators of the first humanoids understood far more about souls, incarnation, and physical death of a body and the soul's return home than we humans do about animals we clone. In fact, few of the scientist cloners of animals even consider the soul that is needed to operate the physical body the process creates.

The ET visitor miners on Earth were admonished severely, precisely because their brethren value human life even more than we humans do, and considered what was done to extract the gold to be a selfish, easy route that did not consider the greater picture.

Human evolution and development have erased the concern, and the growth of billions of souls has resulted from it.

Time has come for both Earth society development and the physical forces and energies now transforming Earth to bring our ET cousins closer to us and more into our awareness. It is time for us to begin joining the community of which we are a part yet do not know we belong.

Do you still regret buying the book? I doubt anyone would read to the end of the first chapter before purchasing it. If you did, you win the Reader Due Diligence Award of the Week and you are in the minority. I apologize for regrets, if you have any; book printers and publishers do not work free. If books were offered on a "Satisfaction Guaranteed or Your Money Back" basis, there probably wouldn't be any. If on the other hand you're glad you've plowed in this deep, eleven more chapters await.

- 2 -
What Is Channeling?

In two words, channeling is telepathic communication.

Letters, syllables, words, sentences, paragraphs, and communication are a human invention. Physical bodies, vocal chords, and ears, not to mention a brain to operate them, are required. A common, nearly universal human belief is of the continued existence of the spirit or soul after physical life. Disagreement with the application and effects of religion give rise to disbelief; the limits of physical bodies reinforce skepticism.

Do sounds not exist if not heard? By that measure, dogs live a greatly expanded existence compared to humans. Do the sun and moon cease to exist after setting? Do food ingredients not exist if invisible? Because decaffeinated coffee looks like the regular stuff means it's the same?

All humans can communicate telepathically. Outside the severely ill or incapacitated, all of us have the ability to incorporate it. This word—supplied by my GAGs (guardian angel guides), nicknamed "The Committee"—literally means "in a body," and telepathy is as natural to you as an elbow on an arm.

Some of us run faster than others, some can barely walk. Some are polyglots, some barely manage their native tongue. As with any talent, great differences in ability exist with channeling. Make no mistake, however; channeling ability exists for all of us, even the biggest of skeptics.

For all of my life, at least all of the adult part until several years ago, I believed most people were given information the way I am. Because no medium, psychic, or channeler (pick your preferred term) occupies another soul's body and brain, I can't say what happens inside anyone else's thoughts—unless invited—and so it was automatic to believe other people's information ebbed and flowed more or less the same for them as it does with me.

I've discovered that's not the case.

Telepathic communication resembles radio waves. We all transmit; among humans there are NO exceptions. NONE.

Human belief requires proof of receipt as evidence. Just as broadcasts aren't received if TV or radio sets are off or not tuned in, telepathic communication sent to a specific person or place requires the recipient to be both "tuned in" and willing and able to acknowledge.

Human social training discourages this ability, in some cases dismissing or even condemning it. Yet it is always there.

Just as there are many types and brands of motor vehicles or specialties among doctors, so are there great differences among mediums.

Some specialize in personal, one-on-one readings with deceased relatives. Some contact lost pets; some issue predictions. Some are accurate in one area, vague in others. Some are frauds.

My preferred application is writing about Earth, human society, and humankind's place in the galaxy.

There are common misconceptions, and I list eight of them below with my explanations. There is no suggestion the general readership of this book holds any of these; however, some might. These could help before proceeding to chapter 3.

Misconception #1: *The future is fixed, and a good psychic can predict it.*

All humans have free will and the ability to choose. Always. There are many nearly certain events because the choice has already been made. That does not mean it is fixed, only that it is unlikely to be changed by you, regarding what will happen to you.

#2: *If it is possible to know x, y, and z, then tell me the name of my dead cat. You can't? Then x, y, and z are also wrong.*

There is little value in getting information from a psychic or medium about what is already known. Such information serves one erroneous purpose, to convert everything into human three-dimensional terms under the belief that existence operates everywhere the same way it does on Earth and for humans.

#3: *Dead relatives are just who I remember. If what I'm getting doesn't match what I know, it's wrong.*

Dead relatives are no longer the relative remembered. A soul might choose to reappear and present what was her- or himself, or might not. No medium or psychic controls this.

#4: *What does he/she/it "look" or "sound" like?*

Not all mediums or psychics get visual imagery. None get words exactly the way humans use them, unless the spirit or soul chooses to communicate to the medium or psychic that way, in the surroundings common to Earth and humans.

#5: *"Past" and "future" lives flow along in a linear timeline, like "everything" else.*

Time, its measurement and sensations on Earth *apply only here*. It doesn't, for a New York second, mean time is NOT relevant on Earth; it is, *absolutely*. As soon as we deal with spirits or entities not bound to Earth bodies or existence, time as humans perceive it can be suspended, reversed, compressed, and expanded. Your past and/or future lives on Earth *are simultaneous* from the place of your soul.

#6: *Channeling feels like ...*

What is it like to eat an apple? The best description ever offered in human language cannot come halfway close to creating the sensation. If you've never eaten one, ask someone who has to describe it. Then bite into one yourself. If you like apples, you already know what words can never re-create.

I can't describe what "channeling" is like; I used to believe it was all my own thoughts. Many people do not identify the distinction; their ability often lies a bit dormant. "Time" came for me to be nudged by my GAGs to begin employing the ability and soon I realized, it is the method or means by which I know and receive information and detail, what society's training had taught me to discount and dismiss.

I thought I was "remembering" but I couldn't recall where, realizing eventually, this is because there was no "where" or "when."

#7: *Mediums can provide information in many languages ...*

Language is a human tool. Consider mute and/or deaf people who use signing to communicate. Are there French and German versions? Deaf mute people literate in one written language can easily communicate with other "signers" either illiterate or able to read and write only in a very different language (*think Chinese and Russian*).

Mediums transliterate information that does not come in words, ordered in the way humans speak or read them. The sender does not create language ability or replace the human brain of the medium. The operation and limits to cerebral function remain in effect for all human psychics and mediums.

#8: *Any unknown information about anything can be gotten from a medium.*

No; the universe and our slice of it are not automatically and instantly connected to everything, and where there are connections, it is only by mutual agreement. Our GAGs play a large part in managing agreements and limitations humans make in their life contracts and plans. These are unique to everyone.

- 3 -
Let's Talk with One

Here I ask questions (*Q:*) about what aliens or extraterrestrials are and what spirits are. What are the similarities, differences, if any, and how does all of it relate to humanity on Earth? I turn to The Committee (*C:*).

The previous chapter is now put into practice. The following suggestion comes from a reader of the author's website, and there will be more such questions in the next chapter.

Reader Question:I have a vibe/inkling if you will, to ask for an interview with an alien, being an extraterrestrial if you will. About us earthlings and our shift in consciousness.

This is a good, nonspecific reader question that leaves open the floor (the screen?) for a variety of questions. Let's see who appears. From here on, "Q:" will preface my questions, answers labeled "AE:" for our alien extraterrestrial.

Q: *Calling all spaceships, calling all spaceships, be on the lookout for ... humans making contact! Most of us, no, but one receiver and many more tuned in to the signals received.*

Silence, so far.

Q: *Any takers?*
AE: Yes, of course.

Q: *Welcome to Earthdom.*
AE: Thank you and we say, here we are. Already.

Q: *Can you tell us where here is, for you?*
AE: Earth.

Q: *Do you receive many requests for contact?*
AE: This is the first. For me and us.

Q: *Do extraterrestrial visitors like contact from humans?*

AE: Yes, it is very rare, most who know of us do not choose this method or medium, it not occurring to them it could be done. The potential believers, and we say potential for reasons we shall explain, desire the contact, however, on terms and under conditions they prefer, within their expected view and projected experience. This will not happen and so the contact occurs not.

Q: *You, or y'all as we might say 'round these parts where I live, have a sound and a rhythm like the one we get from my Committee GAGs. Is this a coincidence?*

AE: No, you are transducing electromagnetic energy we transmit, as do your guardians. As do our guardians. This is adapted, more or less, to your communication code. Thus a similarity of rhythm, because your language has characteristics or limits, from our view, that create the rhythmic pace you detect.

Q: *Please explain "potential believers" in the question before the last one.*

AE: Humans in many ways adore the idea of our appearance, however as humans have often seen in films, and often engaged in activity in response, which dominate human imagery. We might physically resemble some depictions of some extraterrestrials; however, there are many groups of visitors to Earth. Much different. Our ships and vessels we likely will not display, rather we shall send small, what you name, scout ships. Our larger vessels are not appropriate for the Earth environment.

Q: *Why not?*

AE: Size.

Q: *What's the problem there? It's a big sky.*

AE: Fear. The image will create fear only and no purpose shall be served.

Q: *From where are you?*

AE: From which place in the universe you ask?

Q: *Yes!*

AE: The Milky Way you have called it, our galaxy. Our home is a solar system and in the case of this vessel and my fellow travelers, one planet in the system; however, we use several of the systems.

Q: *Where is it?*

AE: We are from the opposite quadrant to yours, from the center of it, approximately. You do not know the stars and obviously not the planets; you cannot yet detect them.

Q: *Could we identify the stars and why did you say it in plural, for two or more?*

AE: The cluster; Earth's star is a cluster member also but the distances between the cluster members do not create the notion or idea yet for Earth. As the ability to travel the galaxy is demonstrated, you will then see what we detect, the star clusterization which is common.

Q: *Is your home a solar system with one specific central star?*

AE: Yes.

Q: *What name do you have for your planets or solar system of planets and star?*

AE: For the solar system, no name as is the case with you on Earth. Our planet we call Nameeda, if we could translate the word to words spoken.

Q: *Do you speak with words to communicate?*

AE: No. No longer. It was done previously.

Q: *How does your planet's cycle of rotation and sunlight compare to Earth, or Mars or even Venus?*

AE: It is the same. However, if you brought a timepiece of Earth, you would discover the segments of the day you use, two parts of twelve each, would not match the dayrise to dayrise cycle. We believe it would be shorter on Nameeda by comparison, but not much.

Q: *Have you measured and prepared Earth specifications? Diameter, atmosphere, composition, etc.?*

AE: Yes, we know more about Earth than you do, about your physical properties.

Q: *Do you know what Earth looks like inside all the way to the core?*

AE: We know the composition. We have not looked by the boring of a hole; however, this isn't needed.

Q: *How are you able to know?*

AE: Each substance has a resonant frequency and likewise an atomic signature, this you know well on Earth also. Each substance also transmits subatomic energy; we suggest a nuclear explosion of the horribly messy and sloppy type you have done on Earth; this is called radiation and involves the subatomic particles. Radiation sickness is the massive overdose, as these particles and the subatomic energy perforate and damage the atomic structure of everything they penetrate.

This subatomic energy transmits a pattern much as does a glowing object through infrared light. This pattern perforates all surrounding matter and can be read; it can be seen by color or mathematic formula.

Q: *How can a formula be measured or seen?*
AE: The Geiger counter known on Earth, which produces an audible click for each particle departing the measured substance, is a hint. This device measures the subatomic particle, the neutron or proton and energy surrounding it which is thrown off the radioactive substance. We have devices that likewise count the frequency waves, much as a frequency of energy on Earth is known to exist. You would call this a resonant frequency and that is correct; the resonance is the frequency level of the material at the atomic and supra-atomic level you detect on Earth. The energy signature from within likewise transmits an energy pulsation, the frequency waves from which can be counted. This image penetrates and as you would say, shines through to any observer that chooses to see it.

Q: *So you can look into Earth and see what's there and how far in?*
AE: Yes.

Q: *What's there?*
AE: Earth is composed of what you believe it contains, but the proportions are not as you think. The iron and steel core, for iron is more prevalent near the surface, deep inside Earth the material is more like the steel you produce on the surface, and is not as large as often depicted. It is of a diameter you would call one thousand kilometers, approximately. The outer edge of this steel core is defined by a sharp interface or border. This substance is liquid by comparison to the surface density and is the origin, the source of Earth's magnetism.

Q: *What keeps it molten?*
AE: It has always been liquid, the radiant energy not allowed to escape because of the surrounding material.

Q: *I have been told by my guardians and guides that Earth surface heat emanates largely from within Earth, and the daily heating and cooling of the surface caused by sunlight and the changing angles only affect Earth down to a certain depth.*
AE: This is correct. We suggest you think of the surface temperature variation of Earth as eddy currents within a much larger flow.

Q: *So if the heat emanates from within and rises to the solid surface, why don't we have a generally cooling effect? What keeps the center of Earth hot?*
AE: Magnetism, both generated and received. The example we would use are your coils for sparks, in automobiles, your transportation

devices. The magnetic field expands then collapses around the coil. The introduction of electricity into a coil creates the magnetism, which then collapses onto the coil as the electricity is interrupted, and a spark is made. Earth magnetism does this also, with the steel and iron Earth contains. The magnetism of the sun, your star has great effect on this. Remember, as your guardians have told you, most of Earth's solid surface is covered by water and the effects of surface heating and cooling are limited to hard land, a small portion of the surface creates the season effects. The vast portions of water absorb the surface heating effect with almost no consequence. The rise of heat to the hard surface under water has little short-term effect on climate and weather; it does control the patterns of Earth surface weather.

Q: *We've been told before, global warming or climate change is not a human effect.*

AE: No, it is not and humans cannot yet affect climate and weather. Magnetism does this.

Q: *OK, so what's inside Earth for the remaining 11,700 kilometers of its diameter, the remaining 92 percent?*

AE: What you call rock. It begins nearly immediately over the surface of the molten center and extends to the surface.

Q: *The crust, what we call the upper layer, is not different from what is found below?*

AE: It is a mixture of many things, all of which are found below. The appearances of many rocks on the surface are the inner materials poking through, as you might say.

Q: *Where does the oil come from?*

AE: This material is contained down to depths impossible to be reached. In some cases it is located one thousand kilometers from the surface; it is simply a residual formation of material like any found in the surface of the Earth.

Q: *Crude oil is not the result of dinosaurs and other vegetative material from millions of years ago?*

AE: In a very few cases, yes; however, they are very few. The majority of oil found deeper than a hundred or two hundred meters is a residual coagulation of material not absorbed by the surrounding rock, much of which is softer than at the surface, if not also liquid.

Q: *How much of Earth's volume is liquid, not hard solid?*

AE: About two-thirds.

Q: *Holy bat cave, Batman! Two-thirds?!?*
AE: Yes, approximately.

Q: *OK, just one more geology question; does any of this matter to humans?*
AE: No, not yet.

Q: *Not yet?*
AE: Not for many generations and lives to come, a dozen we shall suggest as the minimum. Be not concerned in the least way for this.

Q: *How do you communicate?*
AE: As we are doing with you now.

Q: *How can you understand my questions?*
AE: We read them, after your thoughts that create them.

Q: *How far away from me are you, physically?*
AE: In a straight or curved line? We are above your planet at an altitude of what you would consider six hundred kilometers or three hundred fifty miles. Just above your atmosphere.

Q: *It doesn't extend that high, does it?*
AE: No, and the gap is what we consider just above. This gap is tiny, by our estimation. The space for parking a car on your surface is also very small as it relates to a large truck.

Q: *Are you above me?*
AE: No, we are above what you call on Earth, the Indian Ocean.

Q: *Why that location? Any reason?*
AE: The view we like, a huge continent with great mountains and beauty in them and many interesting events of humans below.

Q: *How large is your ship, the one you're in?*
AE: By Earth measurements, its length is approximately 436 meters and width approximately two-thirds this, being a wide oval shape. Depth top to bottom as you would understand this, nearly two hundred meters. Oblong is the word you would use.

Q: *How long is required to travel from your planet Nameeda to Earth?*
AE: By your Earth time, two hours and one-half.

Q: *Do you come to stay for long periods of Earth time or is this a quick trip made often?*
AE: There is not much pattern. We observe as long as we deem it useful,

and this often depends upon the Earth events we see. An example we give; as this session with us you have, there was a recent event in Paris of violence and a march in protest by many world leaders. This is not common and is of great significance and we dare not depart and miss a close-up view of it.

Q: *Are you able to know what happens on Earth from Nameeda?*
AE: Yes, and the transmission delay is similar to the physical distance traversed; to see into what occurs requires the image to be transmitted much as we would travel in the physical. We do not want to be in transit as something major developed, if we could observe it live, with sound and smell and perception of Earth. The Earth example we offer is a television device you use versus in-person viewing. Which is preferable? We can also detect sound and anything else your senses pick up from our perch just above Earth. We can only gain image delays from Nameeda.

Q: *What do you call your race?*
AE: Nameedians, if you will.

Q: *What do you look like?*
AE: We are grayish pale with a subtle violet or purple tinge, in certain moments or situations. Our bodily chemistry is similar to yours, carbon based. Many others in the galaxy and universe are silicon based.

Q: *Are you bipeds, with four limbs, two arms, legs, and a head above a torso?*
AE: Yes.

Q: *How big are you, by comparison?*
AE: We are nearly twice the size on average, our body proportions are not the same, we have longer legs, the lower ambulatory limbs and our arms are also longer. Our neck and head parts are similar yet the cranium is larger and taller. Our brains are similar to yours in size. Smaller in proportion to the body, in other words.

Q: *If the skull or cranium is larger and the brain is the same size, what else is there?*
AE: Bone and cartilage.

Q: *Your head is then heavier as a proportion to your body weight?*
AE: No, about the same as a human, but we are varied in sizes and configurations as are humans.

14

Q: *Do you have hair or wear clothes?*

AE: No and sometimes, sometimes not. Our planet is far dimmer by the amount of sun energy that reaches the surface and our eyes are much larger, to allow intake of the lesser light. We enjoy the sunlight or starlight effects, as your language might say, and the warmth sensation upon the skin. The human traits of modesty are not common on Nameeda.

Q: *Why do you come to observe Earth?*

AE: It is fascinating.

Q: *You mentioned the Paris events and protests, do you see anything coming from these events?*

AE: Of course, we are aware of the many ways your choices could direct events one way or the other, and this fascination with your choices and outcomes draws us in.

Q: *Do you have an opinion about it all?*

AE: Observations we have and we say, the fear of opinion that drives the acts is amazing to see. The disagreement felt that generates the idea to attack is amazing. The attackers feel the need to commit violence because of dislike. No threat comes to their well-being and none they see; they fear not anything will happen to them yet are driven to kill for depiction of ideas. This is amazing to watch and the suggested reactions and responses are likewise amazing.

Q: *Do you see other things humans could do differently?*

AE: Yes, of course. However, no scientist acts upon the urge to direct subjects of research, this will ruin the process. We would never express approval, disapproval, or suggest courses of action any more than one of you would tell the residents of another city what to eat. Well, we see, some of you would and often do this, but that is intra- and interhuman development. Never would we do this.

Q: *How many extraterrestrial ships are near Earth now?*

AE: In this very moment that you ask, we say approximately three dozen large central ships from elsewhere and many, many more smaller observer and scout ships in the atmosphere. This would be two hundred or so.

Q: *Holy crap, that many?!?*

AE: Yes, and there are often many more, both above and in the atmosphere.

Q: *Why don't we see them?*

AE: Often you do and you label one another as crazy and demented, and several of you prance and prattle about proof when the appearance is suggested. It is amazing to observe a debate about us.

Q: *Why don't you just show yourselves and get it over with?*
AE: Yes, why not? What will this achieve?

Q: *I don't know but I am not particularly interested in seeing ETs.*
AE: We know, thus we contact you. We should say, we allow it.

Q: *Are there other ETs of other civilizations listening in on this conversation?*
AE: All of them, yes. Many.

Q: *What do they think?*
AE: Not much, we are not saying anything they do not know well, and many
      have also made contact with humans either telepathically as we are
      doing now, or also physically. They are keen to see the effects on other
      humans who read this, and the interest lies there. For us also.

Q: *Does the president of the USA know about ETs?*
AE: Yes, with absolute certainty.

Q: *How are you so certain?*
AE: We have watched him meet with some. We should say, we have
      watched him be confronted by them.

Q: *He didn't want the contact?*
AE: It was not his choice and never was the choice of any world leader,
      either previous US president or any other leader of a sovereign nation
      or region.

Q: *Region being ... ?*
AE: Roman and Ottoman Empires, for example. All leaders in these regimes
      have met with extraterrestrials, within the context the visitors knew
      they would be understood.

Q: *What do you mean context they would understand?*
AE: Display of flight is permissible to those already accepting it. No
      displays of technology beyond examples already seen on Earth are
      done, to not confuse and erode any chance for credibility. No scout
      ships were shown to Caesar, who knew not what they were.

Q: *What about Greek mythology? Many examples of winged men and
      other such stuff abound. Atlas holding the Earth, yada yada yada.*
AE: Small distant examples of some things have been revealed to humanity
      in this latest development of civilization but much of what we could
      display to humanity has already been shown and is remembered.

Q: *What about the president of the USA? What has he seen?*

AE: Several extraterrestrial representatives.

Q: *Where has he met with them?*

AE: Military bases.

Q: *Why there?*

AE: These surround him with protection and create a sense of calm, by virtue of the capability for force humans hold in these locations. He and many like him of many sovereign nations also understand that extraterrestrial appearances in these locations suggest the defense capability humans have is essentially useless.

Q: *How could ETs penetrate a military base secured for a world leader to be there?*

AE: Easily; simply cloak yourself, rise above then descend in. Unless there is a solid dome above, it cannot be stopped.

Q: *OK, three or four ... what, Pleiadians? They decide to visit a US Marine Corps base in Hawaii while the president of the USA is there on vacation. They suddenly appear where? How do they prevent attack?*

AE: The risk of attack is neutralized electromagnetically, from both the scout ship and the main interstellar ship. This locks the trigger of a firearm and likewise suspends it in place inside an electromagnetic bubble. Even if the tool were discharged, fired as you say, the slug would be seized upon exit from the tube and dropped in place.

Q: *How do you stop the troops from doing other things?*

AE: Simply encase them or anything inside what you call a force field, and lock them in place.

Q: *Do you explain yourselves?*

AE: We Nameedians have not, we have not made this human contact although we could. The other ET visitors calmly explain themselves and what is happening. The protection surrounding the person and person ETs wish to meet is incapacitated. No pain or discomfort occurs, and quickly the intent is established as not hostile.

Q: *What purpose do ETs have in meeting with world leaders?*

AE: Explain the sentiments and desires of humanity, and the portions of it with which the leaders are aligned.

Q: *The leaders don't know this?*

AE: They do; however, their priorities often don't place these atop the list. We have seen some ETs take the role of explaining humanity to leaders.

We suggest an example; a very rich person not given to great philanthropy certainly knows it is possible and can easily pursue it. It would erode a good deal of the wealth the rich person possesses and, for this reason and others, is often not followed. This is a choice of humanity, to transfer wealth and allow the accumulation of riches, to value these riches and to act upon receipt of them. Free will to act is the prime directive of humanity, and the ETs meeting with leaders often hope to show leadership where they can work to enhance the free will of the people supporting them.

Q: *Do you believe the message gets through?*
AE: Yes; however, action comes very slowly.

Q: *Could leaders act faster?*
AE: Yes, or not at all. ETs provide an option and view the contacting ETs as useful, helpful, and beneficial. What is done with this information depends on the listener.

Q: *Of the dozens of ET civilizations observing Earth close by ...*
AE: And many more from afar ... "on screen" as you would say.

Q: *... how many contact humans openly and regularly?*
AE: Just a few.

Q: *Reason?*
AE: To not overwhelm, and no good purpose is served by it.

Q: *What is the fascination of observing humanity?*
AE: Look upon your Earth; how much land do you know well? Great portions of the Earth's dry surface are not well known or are barely understood. The oceans remain a great unknown. How fascinated and fixated would you become with the knowledge and treasures of sea life and geography, if you could just descend to the depths of the oceans, illuminate what is there, and study it? For us, observing Earth, human behavior, emotion, interaction, and the effects upon the environment and vice versa are, as you would call, a treasure trove of insight and understanding of the universe.

Q: *Is Earth that unique physically?*
AE: Yes, it is a rare bird in the galaxy and universe.

Q: *Do all ETs have physical bodies and souls, lifetimes and death and guardians and guides watching over them?*
AE: Yes, to a great extent. There are variations among the many civilizations; however, they are not immense.

Q: *What is the lifespan of a "person" in your civilization?*
AE: By your time on Earth, several hundred years.

Q: *Is humanity crude?*
AE: No. There are elements of human behavior and ways we could call rudimentary by contrast elsewhere in the galaxy, but crude? No. Not at all.

Q: *The challenges of the Earth environment at large? They seem that way for us, we who make it and live it?*
AE: The opportunities are enormous, and you all take great advantage. One great opportunity presented is the capacity to criticize oneself and others, then see beyond it and learn to turn the critical view into an analytical one. We have no such capacity for bitter condemnation as some humans display with great skill. It is wonderfully valuable to be the object of such attacks; it feels horrible and gives so much.

Q: *Why don't ETs land a ship on Earth, get out, and explain themselves live and on the BBC?*
AE: This is an excellent question and we shall simply say, because if that were done, too many humans would insist upon a leadership role for the arrivers. Suddenly the idea a higher power can override what exists now would be grabbed and held so closely to the chest of humanity you would suffocate yourselves. Humans want solutions delivered, and some are very given to delivering those solutions. Oppressors they become.

We are not given to lie to you; we would soon be asked to cure cancer. We can eradicate this disease in a human already suffering from it, to nearly the fatal phase of the condition. Unlikely we would be successful in reversing the effects in a person with just a few weeks of human time remaining, who has long suffered the disease. Anyone else in a stage prior to this could have the effects halted. The longer the disease has affected the victim, the lower the likelihood all effects would be reversed to a complete recovery, but in many cases, our treatment would eliminate it from the person struck, in weeks to months to never return.

We will not set fire to your houses and will not drop bombs upon your cities, in this way. You do not see our ability to eradicate cancer as a conflagration. It would be.

Our display of the ability to neutralize weapons will do two things immediately; it would cause some of you to insist we provide it as a means to stop harm. The requesters, themselves possessing weapons, would not want their own weapons rendered useless in return for our neutralization of the adversary's weaponry. Other forces on Earth would desire all weapons be eliminated and we say, this we could do. Simply supply a list of what you consider a weapon.

There are many things able to be employed as one, some designed for other purposes. Electricity for light is good; to electrocute a condemned inmate to death, as a sentence for a crime, is not good for that person. In that circumstance, a weapon it is. Does your list contain electricity as a weapon? Lightning is far more lethal than gunfire, but your inability to cause it would leave it outside the definition.

The human desire to see our ability to eradicate weaponry quickly leads to our need to referee then control the acts and emotions that lead to the use of the weapons. No knife cuts without a human grasping, slashing, and thrusting. So what would be thrust in place of the knife? After eradication of weapons, would we eradicate emotion? Behavior?

Our appearance on Earth would lead swiftly to this development, as you can see.

Burn down your civilization we shall not; block your roads through life we cannot and thus we stand down and stand away from our presence.

Q: *Will humanity reach a point of acceptance without some aspects of human society going off the rails at the appearance of ETs?*
AE: Yes, some already do. The large question that must be answered is, why do you want to see ETs on Earth? This question requires great introspection few have taken time to conduct; just as the hungry, wailing baby does so as reaction to the hunger, to signal his parents and caretakers that it must eat. This small child has no ability in its infancy to introspect, yet feels strongly the sensation and reacts vigorously.

This same dynamic operates with many a human, its source unexamined and not understood yet. We are unwilling to supply the spark to the fuse we understand exists.

Q: *I have personally never felt much fascination or desire to see ETs and wonder why sometimes.*
AE: You are more introspected and do not remember it.

Q: *I would love to interpret ETs for others, in a way we are doing now.*
AE: You can do so all you like, where others will listen. Will they?

Q: *What I mean is in a live, in-person Q&A session.*
AE: Assemble your audience, we will answer any question or explain why we cannot or do not explain.

Q: *I don't know how to do it and don't feel much urge to do so.*

AE: Then allow others to make the arrangement and contact you.

Q: *OK, it would be a lot of fun and faster than typing.*

AE: Yes.

Q: *Do ETs live as we do, with families, challenges, threats, joy, sadness, and happiness as we do on Earth?*

AE: Yes, all of these things and more.

Q: *Have the ET civilizations that visit eliminated violence and strife?*

AE: Yes, almost completely.

Q: *Why can't we do it on Earth?*

AE: You can and may and allow no one to suggest it isn't possible or quickly. You may do so with immediate effects. Inside two generations Earth society would no longer resemble itself. Bear in great mind, the opportunity cost would not be low; however, the investment would deliver a great return. You would lament the cost of the lost opportunities.

The pet dog so loved will always be remembered no matter how many great and beloved dogs come to a family after the first one dies.

As humanity quickly chose to behave toward elimination of strife and conflict as now occur, the benefit of lessons learned through them would be missed, as is the long-lost family pet.

Q: *What then can we do when we see something horrible happen?*

AE: Match it to appreciation of something you have and like, but are not immediately thinking about. Upon witnessing a horrible violent death, think of a beautiful person you love who is alive.

Q: *What do world leaders think of the ETs that visit? Why don't the world leaders get bypassed, and contact is not made with greater humanity?*

AE: Who chose the leaders and how are they not you? We say, your governments and kings and queens and ministers and presidents and dictators and … choose your label, they are you. You create the roles and then you fill them.

Who are we to tell you otherwise, to arbitrarily discard what you choose to do, with great energy and gusto?

Has any one person in a nation where elections occur not seen the energy given to the process of acquiring leadership and governing with it? Who are we to say humanity should not do this? It is not our choice to do it, it is not our place to interfere, and NEVER is it our place to agree with your assertion that humanity and leadership are separate.

To your first question, we contact humanity, some of us, regularly. Do we not do this now? How many among you would discount and discard this whole thing as a fantasy? We have no control over this reaction, this idea, and this view.

The some who say a person offering contact with an ET is crazy are as entitled to the right to express notions and opinions of sanity and craziness as they are to define their idea of normality. The right of expression for the one means it is for the all.

World leaders are apprehensive of the contact, for they dislike the uncontrol. We seek no control, the few who visit and make contact, and will not allow it. We come hands open, arms outstretched, and minds open. Because we display great power some of us—and we all possess it—the fear is just under the surface that we will misuse it.

World leaders, especially the more powerful among humans, who have great military force at their disposal, are uneasy with a force that suspends their ability at a literal snap of the fingers.

Q: *Do ET civilization have weapons?*
AE: Yes, for defense; however, these abilities are largely mental. There are some physical capabilities, and these are the only ones suggested and used. Earth offensive capability is all easily suspended electromagnetically where a threat to an ET is possible.

Q: *Isn't it possible to sneak up on an ET and attack?*
AE: No, for the thoughts of this act are read like a book. We can simply avoid it, before it can be manifested, or neutralize it before any harm comes to anyone. This alarms world leaders.

Q: *Does your civilization on Nameeda use names?*
AE: For things, yes; however, not for ourselves very often. We use codes for things like addresses, our locations and bases, and identification. Taking away the name and assigning a number, you could say. Names in alphabets are just numbers anyway, so little change is there. This allows easy and complete lists.

Q: *How many live on your planet?*
AE: About three billion.

Q: *How large is it?*
AE: By Earth measurement it is approximately 50 percent larger in diameter and has also abundant liquids on the surface.

Q: *Water?*
AE: Yes.

Q: *Are all organisms carbon chemistry based?*
AE: No, there are also silicon-based organisms, mostly the vegetative matter.   Green plants of Earth are largely blue. The water is reddish in color, where Earth water appears blue.

Q: *What is the atmosphere's composition?*
AE: Similar to Earth, less oxygen, however, the planet is flatter and almost no higher altitude living there is. The oxygen content is similar to your mountains at five to eight thousand feet, one thousand four hundred to two thousand five hundred meters. There is less nitrogen and more carbon dioxide.

Q: *How are you able to extract nutrition from silicon-based vegetation with carbon-based bodies?*
AE: This answer is too long for this forum, yet we will say, Earth understanding of biochemistry is limited to Earth possibilities. It is done as easily as Earth nutrition and sustenance are accomplished.

Q: *When will humanity see regular, open, and unmistakable visits of ETs?*
AE: Already. How obvious need it be? More than now occurs, we shall say with certainty, to convince the greater population.

It will be more obvious and we suggest in several years, beginning in a bigger way this year of your calendar two thousand fifteen. We must caution, bigger by what percentage? So little of what now occurs is acknowledged, a 10 or 15 percent increase will not likely raise the awareness or acceptance among the many of you.

We understand the civilizations now making regular contact and often with government and military leadership might do it without provoking much response, because these leaders already understand there is little reason to have fear and, moreover, there is nothing they can do to prevent it. However, what explanation will the population expect?

If this happens openly away from seats of government, many people will demand at least an explanation or a response. What response can be offered that has not already been given the ETs? None we say.

What explanation? That leadership has been receiving these contacts for decades but not disclosed it? Do you wish to have leadership state the existence of a many decades-long cover-up? We assure you, you will not among the majority of you, be pleased with this. Your leaders, elected or otherwise, thrive on power and popularity and will do much to maintain it through imagery perceived to sustain satisfaction.

You are your governments, they are you, they reflect you, you create them, and you control them. You also control your sensation you cannot.

Your leadership largely believes it knows better and can better do for you what you cannot collectively achieve, and proceeds with this idea. This is always the case and would be reinforced through the instinctive reaction most people would demand.

In the USA the population would demand an opinion and position; would none be offered? This would not propagate confidence and would undermine credibility, something no government wants to show and no populace wants to see. So a position would be offered, but it would largely be a façade.

What does this achieve for humanity?

ETs are unwilling to circumvent humanity in a large way; we are respectful of your decision because we hope and want you to be respectful of ours. We must always proceed in this way, and always have.

We make regular contact and hope the contacted are not badly affected by our decision to do so, if they choose to reveal it. The many of you, although the few reading this, are quick to label anyone as crazy. This comes easily and sadly to humanity.

The vim and vigor expressed by the demanders of proof who are unable to state definitively what proof they shall accept runs rough over the new idea so uncomfortable. The personalization of attacks is well understood and this slows our desire to disclose the existence of our beings.

The Flat Earth Society operates under a new management and premise still.

Q: *This sounds like a collective communication from many ETs, not just you Nameedians.*
AE: Correct, we have channeled thoughts from the many observing.

Q: *What name do I use to thank you?*
AE: Call me Nameedian One and you have; you are welcome. Your
         Committee asks that we return to visit if requested, both to Earth
         orbit and to your questions.

Q: *That would be good, as soon as I think of some! So long for now ...*
AE: Good-bye.

- 4 -
More Examples

Now that channeling or telepathic communication has been demonstrated, here are some more sessions done with ETs.

Q: *Extraterrestrials have physical bodies like us, right?*

C: Similar in structure and composition, yes. How much they are like you, in your way of understanding similarity, you would decide. We say yes, you might say otherwise.

Q: *What differences are there?*

C: They are what your biology calls bipeds, with two legs for movement and also two limbs for all other uses, beyond location and movement. The sizes of eye organs and the placement are larger; the quantities of light from stars allows this and encourages it. The cerebral organs and skulls are also often larger than yours and you shall find larger- and smaller-sized bodies. Coloring is different; the presence of copper and silicon, where iron and carbon are found on Earth bodies, creates a difference in hue. There is much less body hair, often very little.

Q: *Are these differences mostly environmental?*

C: The environment and conditions are a factor. However, development of society is also a large reason for the differences. Physical work humans have traditionally done is unique.

Q: *Many stories and fables about centaurs, mermaids, and other mythical creatures suggest strange biological combinations that would be created by whom?*

C: These combinations existed on Earth, created through ability to manipulate your DNA codes. As Atlantis was destroyed, so was the technology and soon desire and ability to create the torso of a human on the body of a horse.

Q: *Are our computer codes part of this?*

C: They are a basic facsimile of the process, yes.

Q: *I suspect our computer animations and programs mimic what is "manifestation" or creation of physicality from thought; is this right?*

C: Yes.

Q: *So extraterrestrial visitors to Earth travel in ships or vessels across great distances, enter Earth's atmosphere and observe. Do they use protective suits or other gear?*

C: Yes, this is done, and beyond clothing or other suits or outerwear, generally not.

Q: *Do all extraterrestrials have the ability to breathe our atmosphere?*

C: No; however, visitors that venture onto the surface, yes.

Q: *What are the thinking differences?*

C: Spoken communication is rare; however, vocal chords for it are sometimes, if rarely used. Ears and sound detection are common, just as sounds have great meaning to you and all animals on Earth, so do your visitor cousins derive great benefit from detection of sound.

Q: *From how far away can the unspoken communication take place?*

C: It is very close when young, in what you call infancy and the toddler stages of life and expands until the equivalent of puberty or adolescence is reached. Then the ability extends throughout the population on the one or any respective planet.

Q: *Extraterrestrials read our thoughts?*

C: Of course, and you can read theirs if you wish. Just as you can learn another language of your Earth, the effort and inputs are similar.

Q: *When encountering extraterrestrials, we are not able to collaborate secretly?*

C: No.

Q: *OK, then what's a spirit?*

C: No physical body as you and your visitor cousins have.

Q: *Do extraterrestrials also die and go to "Heaven?"*

C: Many of you have lived as these "extraterrestrials," and, yes, just as you do.

Q: *Is there the same isolation and wall of separation for aliens as humans?*

C: Yes, with more doorways, windows, and hatches.

Q: *Can extraterrestrials more easily communicate with their guardian angels and guides? Do they all have them?*

C: Yes and yes, although often a lesser number at any one moment. The efficiency of communication requires less assistance in most circumstances and situations.

Q: *How does a human know the difference?*

C: Your own spirits and guides and angels will communicate with you as you ask and also as they believe good for you; extraterrestrials will not until you ask and request and then only with your permission, through your guides. So if you wish to receive thought communications from extraterrestrials, you would ask. If one or several are available and willing, they shall answer you. This is rare as the proportion of humans to visitors does not favor it; the extraterrestrials already know which humans are more open to receive and converse. We say, you have attracted a crowd in this moment, very aware the subject is being discussed.

Q: *Are extraterrestrials just as fascinated with the idea of their own guides and angels?*

C: Yes.

Q: *What is the lifespan of the typical extraterrestrial?*

C: This typical applies not; there are many variations. By the equivalence of your Earth years and time, several hundred; however, time moves not the same for all physical beings of the universe. These concepts mesh not well from the views of the one or the other. The independent observer appreciates the dichotomies of this "time" concept as applicable in the many interpretations.

Q: *Why are humans only now going to see visitor presence? What changed?*

C: Evolution on Earth and energies in the universe.

Q: *Have we evolved well?*

C: You have been placed in the center of a great wilderness with all features of Earth as you know them; forests, valleys, mountains, rivers, plains, and otherwise. You travel outward and eventually reach the edge of the wilderness, which is finite. Which path shall have been taken? Yes, the walk through the valley would be far easier than climbing the mountains and certainly much less interesting. All routes provide great benefit and growth; decisions made along the way and the consequences all provide an interesting experience. The opportunity to return and try again in completely different circumstances allows a rebuilding and upbuilding only possible upon the experience already achieved. Against this each of you shall decide upon a deathbed, a life review, and a life planned what "well evolved" shall mean for each of you, alone.

Q: *Spirits have no physical body?*
C: Not as you understand it, no. The sensations created by the limits of physicality, also no.

Q: *Do aliens benefit from the physical existence as do humans?*
C: At least as much, if not even more. As you all shall, as evolution of physical bodies proceeds on Earth.

Q: *Committee, we thank you.*
C: Our welcome to you all.

***

Another reader of my website asked about ETs in August of 2013.

Reader Question:

> *When are the aliens going to make first contact with the human earthlings? 'We, the human race, are suffering badly, especially our younger generation. The use of sarin in the Syrian war is gut wrenching and saddening. Humanity needs help from the outside world :(*

C: We must clarify the words, as others have said on and to your Earth; alien is foreign to you and many of Earth's inhabitants are alien to you, the animals. Extraterrestrials are visitors from other planets and systems and they are simply off the Earth, not alien to your structure and existence. The similarities will surprise you.

Different body chemistry and appearance is what shall be encountered, the differences lesser by much than encountered between animals of Earth and you, the humans.

Extraterrestrials have been making contact for millions of your Earth years and do it now. We suggest you wish appearance and interaction that shall be similar to the encounter and meeting between all humans.

This will commence in a larger way during the next several years of Earth time; these encounters have already happened and many in your governments have been through the experience of such encounters.

We suggest the most rapid way to increase our presence is to stop caring; give it little importance. It is the focus placed upon this revelation that holds it back, for your fixation will derail your courses and history, materially and detrimentally.

We understand the reaction to our suggestion humans should care little. Yet in your thoughts, you know this to be true; imagine a national election among several tens of millions where only a handful of votes are cast, the constituents on strike, as you would say. No candidate could assume power within a system without votes, the outcome illegitimate.

In this way, providing little attention will bring visits to the peak in short order. We know this is very unlikely; and from great fascination to fear will be expressed.

You suggest the use of gas to kill in the Syrian conflict will be solved by extraterrestrials; does the desire to kill fade with removal of the tool of execution? If extraterrestrials solve this example of genocide, what will resolve the next? Are humans incapable in this way? To suggest abolition of weaponry without explanation to successful defensive users is to say the saved must be sacrificed to please the weaker? You are far stronger than you know.

As the ability to act this way is of Earth, so is it the ability to act another way not also of the Earth? This conflict will resolve when victims choose it. Look to your hearts, not the Heavens, for the escape. It shall emerge and surround you, as you allow.

**

A reader of the author's website submitted an outstanding question, and as I read it, I was flooded with answers, as often happens.

The reader question:

> *"I want to ask why extraterrestrials or other dimensional beings often choose to communicate primarily with those in power or the upper echelon of society? Our government(s) has made choices that are not in the best interest of the US or humanity at large yet aliens are primarily communicating with the top of the hierarchy. We have heard of shared technologies between aliens and our government and information provided regarding possible futures for humanity on small and large scales.*

"We have wealthy and powerful people in control of miraculous technology and creating shelters and other solutions to save themselves in a potential disaster while the common man works tirelessly to make those same people money and is ignorant of all of these covert goings on as most of the knowledge is intentionally kept secret.

"What is the rationale behind communicating explicitly and primarily with the very people who hide and distort information, control outcomes, and fix the system to serve their best interest alone without concern for the majority?

"I understand the concept that humans collectively choose these status quo conditions, but on Earth in 3D daily living, we currently have people in power who are not serving our best interests or the will of humanity despite a desire of many to live a different reality (although in actuality we are all choosing this particular potential). We can appreciate this concept all the while we need an incredible number of people to shift their perspective and choices to make any tangible difference.

"It seems like aliens should inform and communicate with humanity at large to assist in the empowerment of making different choices and creating different outcomes that serve the benefit of the majority. Instead, supposedly, alien beings have been making agreements, contracts (e.g., see Erik's [Erik Rune Medhus; ChannelingErik.com] brief discussion on FEMA camps and contracts with ETs), and information exchanges with those in power who undermine the ultimate outcome of humanity, which is to evolve to a higher plane of consciousness, awareness, and state of being.

"This seems nonsensical."

The Committee:

"We shall speak, as you might say, to each paragraph and then generally to this concept, this view and this question about your cousins who visit you and what we see of these interactions.

"To the first paragraph we do say, your extraterrestrial visitors do not communicate primarily with leadership, and they prefer otherwise. Communication and interaction is common with humans away from leadership. You have each individually and thus collectively chosen to label yourselves as crazy for discussing these interactions. The one of you reading this might say no idea of crazy would you ever assign to your view and perception of another person's discussion of extraterrestrial interaction; however, many, if not all of you, know it is a commonly held view.

"Where communication with Earth society leadership has and does occur indeed has involved exchange, offer, and interaction. Of great respect, what you call ETs choose to follow what humanity has created. One and many ETs now listen and beg the opportunity to yield the floor, pass the microphone, or offer the stage. We believe this useful and so we do."

The microphone is passed on to an extraterrestrial. You know, the ETs, that fantasy skeptics insist do not exist; yeah, those guys. Here we go ... (reader note, this communication was done on the 25th of December 2013):

"Greetings all, on your merry day of Christmas, one and all who might celebrate as does your self-described scribe and generally to all others. My name is Zebulon from Canopus and I live in the flesh as you do. I am now above your planet, in a place you would call in orbit, yet I do not. Our vessel need not orbit by use of Earth's gravity, although possible this is.

"Thank you we do for listening; we honor and respect what you have created. Your human societal hierarchies are your creation. Why should we undermine, circumvent, or avoid them? You suggest we prefer leadership communication over otherwise, and to this we suggest, what would happen if leadership were ignored? Human views of roles, ranks, and placements inside the hierarchies and organizations humans have created are not ours to redefine, interpret to your benefit, and rearrange to suit the ideas of the one against the other.

"A good day we bid you all."

The Committee:

"We return thus to the pulpit and resume. Your government is you, individually and collectively. It is entirely a human creation, why should a human creation be disregarded, cast aside, and ignored? Which one person or group should have the power, authority, or right to suggest we ignore the creation of your collective choice? This your question infers and we say, if this you wish, amass a majority of your fellow citizens to request we sidestep your government hierarchies and we shall.

"The question's second paragraph: how did these individuals become wealthy and who cedes power to them? How are they able to control?

If you wish an example of your control, cease to vote in the next available election. Stay away from the process, observe with interest the attempts incumbents shall make to maintain or seize power under a system nobody has chosen to perpetuate and so you shall see how you supply power and by your choices create the perception of wealth. If you value money yourself, then you grant value to the money another temporarily holds, and the amounts. These accumulate by human choice, solely and completely. Who are we to arbitrate your economic choices, your decisions, and the outcomes?

"Change this system if covert, secret, and self-interests are not to your liking and be always aware that once your interests are attacked to your dislike, will you be so accepting and forgiving of such attempts when, as you commonly say, the shoe is on the other feet?

"As to the third paragraph, this happens not and we do not prefer this, no ET likes this. Such view is human only.

"To the remaining paragraphs we speak generally, and do say ... expect not that we shall interfere in a distortion as you see it. Such misshapes of human society and justice, fairness and equality as we understand you see, are not our place to distort.

"Where should we allow you freedom and where shall we override your will? The collective effect is never to the preference of the entirety; exceptions occur always. When the trend, flow, and result become unpleasant to a majority, we can confidently say, you shall change it yourselves. Your human history of just these past several millennia bear great witness to this, and up comes another moment of such change.

"We thank you for this question, forum, and opportunity to answer and do know it lifts understanding of humanity, understanding of itself and its desires. There comes a time when we shall offer more openly certain information, ideas, and methods but always to your acceptance of them, never to your dislike. Choices made with offerings are always yours, the benefits your property. Detriments or defects that result, your choice also. As no sane humans would deliver weapons to youngsters, we shall not offer up to your risk the technologies you might misuse from inexperience, and we will always keep 'the keys' when such risk rises unacceptably, although this has not happened.

"Be well, we wish you all."

- 5 -
Their Homes

From where do extraterrestrial beings come? Generally, other planets! Well, that's not quite precise; it's more accurate to say, they all come from planets. The majority visiting Earth come from our galaxy, which we've named the Milky Way; however, there are some visitors from other galaxies. More on that in later chapters.

The extraterrestrial beings of our galaxy comprise the vast majority of visitors to Earth, but that does not mean most physical beings or living physical creatures from around the galaxy visit Earth. The vast majority of such animal life does not visit us ever. A good portion of it does not know about Earth and does not have the technology to detect our existence.

Humans also have a difficult time detecting other planets orbiting nearby stars. Nearby means within one hundred or so light years, the distance light would travel during one hundred revolutions of Earth around the sun. The reason is simple and straightforward; insufficient light reflects off them to reach Earth. We could train our most powerful telescopes on the largest of planets and never know it, and we have, haphazardly and unwittingly. We are able to identify the oscillating movement of a star an orbiting planet creates, just as we can measure the oscillation of Jupiter or Saturn's orbit caused by its satellites or moons.

Without a telescope, however, we cannot even see all the planets in our own solar system; the human seven-day week is based on observation of what was visible without optical assistance. The day of the Sun and Moon begin the week (Sun Day and Moon Day) named for our two largest celestial objects. Many languages besides English use the equivalent planet name peculiar to that language, to name the days. Mars is "martes" in Spanish, which also means Tuesday. Martedì is Tuesday (Mars Day) in Italian, Wednesday in Spanish is miércoles, the planet Mercury is mercurio, and Wednesday is mercoledì in Italian. Jupiter represents Thursday, Venus is for Friday and Saturn, our last day of the week, is of course, "Saturn Day."

Maybe if telescopes had been around when the seven-day week was invented, it would have become a nine- or ten-day week; we'd argue nowadays it would have been the metric system multiples or fractions of ten applied to time measurement also.

If we cannot see or otherwise detect planets, there isn't much we can know about them. Earth can be detected by the ET visitors, the very reason they visit. How they do so is explained in chapter 7, but let's discuss what a few examples of planets look like.

Where are these planets from which ETs originate? All of the nearby stars and systems, such as Sirius, Canopus, Pleiades, Alpha Centauri, Barnard's Star, Epsilon Eridani, and many others. There are many stars within fifteen light years of Earth. Light moves at 300,000 kilometers per second in our dimensional range; there are 31,536,000 seconds in one year. Light travels, according to our ability to detect it, 9,460,800,000,000 kilometers in a year. (Nine trillion, four hundred sixty billion, eight hundred million.) Over ten years, the distance is 94.6 trillion kilometers. In galaxial terms, that's not very far; in fact, it's right around the corner. More on this in chapter 7.

From which close stars are there planets that have produced visitors and civilization? Sirius is the major offender, the brightest star in the night sky. It's 8.6 light years away and twice the size of the sun. It has a white dwarf orbiting nearby, which is the size of Earth with the density of our sun. The light we see from Sirius has been en route for longer than it has taken Earth to rotate around the sun 8½ times. Emphasis on the words, "light we can see." Light also moves much faster, in dimensions we cannot detect.

The Alpha Centauri system, with its pair of stars A and B and the nearby Proxima Centauri, is less than half that distance. Astronomers suspect there are planets there, but no confirmation has been made by our telescopes. We'd have to point the best one, the orbiting Hubble Space telescope (unaffected by human surface light or the atmosphere) at also the star itself for literally weeks on end, with the hope we'd see an orbiting planet cross in front of it.

We don't have any telescopic evidence to "prove" there are planets orbiting these stars. We don't have any names for the planets we can't "prove" exist. Zebulon kindly used our Earth name for his nearby star, when identifying himself for this book. I wonder where he came up with his name Zebulon?

Skeptics will doubt I "heard" it and would insist on an audio recording for confirmation; even then they'd doubt the recording's "authenticity." I'm certain they'd say the name was just plucked from the Old Testament. Maybe Zebulon did just that; he didn't "speak" to me in words and I did not "hear" the name with my ears, that's for certain. I've never read the Old Testament as a stand-alone book, just bits and bytes as I've flipped through the New Testament part of the Bible, a two-books-in-one set.

I now ask my guides, The Committee, to describe what planets might be like orbiting just the stars near Earth.

As always, "Q:" are my questions and "C:" are answers from The Committee.

Q: *I am certain both trained and amateur astronomer alike would like a map, accounting, and detailed description from you three, of all the planets of all the stars we have detected close to Earth. I am also certain you won't hand that over, if it were even possible, but you know all of this detail.*

C: We can look up the detail, as you say. We do not dwell on these planets at this moment in your Earth time, we are connected to you on your planet. This is our focus.

To turn our focus away for a moment, we can say there will be found a great variety of planet sizes, conditions, and life forms on all of them as part of the solar systems represented by the stars in just your brief, small section of the galaxy.

Q: *All of the nearby stars have planets?*
C: Nearly all; however, there are a few exceptions. These are not material.

Q: *The planets themselves, what are some of them like?*
C: There are smaller, closer ones with inhospitable conditions for life as you understand animal and plant life to be. Planet formation as a part of the star formation means the larger planets are farther from the star. The size and mass carry more energy and throw them farther from the center until gravitational equilibrium is achieved.

Q: *Gravity equilibrium?*
C: When the forces of gravity of each object pulling them no longer overcome one another.

Q: *What causes a planet to orbit? Why doesn't it just sit there?*
C: It was thrown far from the star when the system was created, from the matter and material which coalesce into what becomes the star and eventual planets. The heavier elements or materials are ejected; as the energy of this propulsion carries the newly formed planet outward, the birthing star, what will become one, exerts a gravitational pull. This curves the outward trajectory, becoming an orbit when the balance or equilibrium of magnetisms are reached.

Q: *Is this how Earth and our solar system were created?*
C: Yes.

Q: *How many civilizations across our galaxy have reached the point of development where they can travel here and back?*

C: Many, many thousands.

Q: *How many ET civilizations or races visit Earth?*

C: Far fewer and on a regular, ongoing basis, approximately three dozen.

Q: *What about nonregular visitors?*

C: Many more; there have been thousands.

Q: *What about the civilizations with selfish interests?*

C: These exist also and are kept away. They are not permitted to approach Earth with capabilities of landing on the surface, for they would likely do so. The manner and method of such landing would immediately create a detrimental distortion.

Q: *It seems to me, one aspect of human society that could use a little improvement is the way responsibility for a reaction is placed on an opinion disliked. Aside from obviously illegal or immoral things, it seems we should refocus responsibility for feeling offended upon the person who chooses to be offended, not just the opinion or person offering ideas, concepts, or making statements. Consistency means the human race should also bear responsibility for our collective reaction to extraterrestrials, and the visitor should not be concerned about how we could react.*

C: The extraterrestrials agree; however, the appearance will be done gradually. Your ET cousins do not want to shock the system. Regular and consistent ET contact was more common on Earth in previous civilizations, when there were far fewer humans on Earth. The telepathic aspects of communication and the nature of your soul's spirituality were more accepted.

Q: *OK, back to the chapter's subject, THEIR homes. What do some of the ET planets look like?*

C: In the case of a binary star, we mention this because you have identified the groups you have named Alpha Centauri and Sirius; there are variations of daylight, day and night cycles and resulting changes. On the planets receiving a regular, varying amount of starlight, there are less acute surface temperature cycles than on your Earth. This less abrupt cyclicality creates less weather system movement over time and generally a cloudier environment. Evaporation of moisture is more even and there are less desert-like or arid areas, and cloud cover is more consistent and even. This has effects on vegetation growth and appearance, and the physical beings also appear different.

Q: *Sticking with the few dozen "regulars," are these visitors the most developed life forms from their respective solar systems?*

C: Yes.

Q: *Are there many solar systems in the galaxy with several inhabited planets where markedly different levels of development have occurred?*

C: Yes, there still are.

Q: *What colors would we see if approaching any of these planets? Earth looks bluish green, with white swirls of clouds and varying beiges and brown of land poking through, with some green mixed in.*

C: There are large portions of green land on Earth, we remind you. The many planets appear in several different colors and combinations. From the surface looking to the atmosphere, you can find the same or very similar blue as Earth; there is a greenish blue also very common, there is green, and there is also a greenish yellow in some cases.

Q: *Mountains? Oceans? Rivers?*

C: All of the surface geological features of Earth are found throughout the galaxy. We must say, Earth is a unique combination, and has a very dense diversity of climates, geographies, and topographies. Earth is not common in the galaxy and is deemed somewhat rare, somewhat unique.

Q: *How about the home planets of the regulars? How do they compare to Earth?*

C: None is as diverse as your planet, physically. There is also less diversity among the plant and animal species, and this includes your ET visitors. The vast array of differences among humans are not as common on these planets. There exist great differences, but not to the same extent as Earth.

Q: *Do these planets all have green plants and chlorophyll?*

C: Many do but not all; there are blue plants on many, where the leaves would appear green on Earth.

Q: *Photosynthesis occurs?*

C: Of course. However, the basic differences in chemistry are carbon and silicon. Human plant and animal life is hydrocarbon, thus carbon based. On many other worlds, the base element is silicon.

Q: *Silicon compounds?*

C: Yes.

Q: *Do animals and plants breathe, exchanging gases the way life on Earth does between oxygen and carbon dioxide?*

C: Yes, atmospheres are present on all planets where civilizations live.

Q: *I looked up silicon compounds out of curiosity and most of them occur on Earth as solids.*
C: There are elements present on many planets that do not exist on Earth. Therefore, many compounds Earth does not know.

Q: *Are there oceans and water on these planets?*
C: Vast amounts. Hydrogen and oxygen are common throughout your galaxy and even the universe. Look at your sun, as an example.

Q: *How bright is sunlight in these other planets?*
C: The intensity of surface light varies from slightly stronger than found on Earth to less than half.

Q: *I assume all of these planets have different rates of rotation and revolution in orbit. Compared to Earth, there is no match between what we'd call a day and what would be a day on another planet.*
C: On many there is also no absolute darkness in the shadow created by the dark side into which a half of the surface is always submerged, on Earth.

Q: *That means they get light from two stars?*
C: Yes, and the amounts rise and fall, but it is always possible to see the surface. We offer your Earth's full moon effect as an example. It reflects enough of your star's light to illuminate the surface.

Q: *If sunlight, or should I say, starlight is always reaching the surface of some of these planets, the growth patterns and rhythms of life must be vastly different.*
C: Yes, and you humans seem as vastly unusual to your visitors as they would seem to you.

Q: *Can a human visit and breathe normally on any of the planets?*
C: Of course. Almost all humans can withstand or adapt to variations in gaseous concentrations on Earth. Just as hemoglobin rises to compensate for less oxygen at altitude, so can variations of nitrogen, carbon dioxide, oxygen, and helium be tolerated without side effects, or with some but not permanently.

Q: *Could humans visit and live on some other planets?*
C: Yes.

Q: *Even though it doesn't deal with ET worlds, this chapter's subject, can some ETs visit Earth and exist or live on the surface?*

C: They can and many have.

Q: *Would the rate of rotation of Earth, light intensity, length of day, or anything else about our environment make a visitor ill or uncomfortable?*
C: Yes, either quickly or over time, depending on which visitor. If a human were brought to a planet orbiting Canopus, you would discover the length of time measured by a battery-powered digital watch to become useless while there. The expectation sunlight would appear with the visibility of the central star, what you call sunrise, after marking twenty-four segments of the Earth cycle would not occur, and soon your physical body rhythms would be disturbed. You would easily solve this by retreating to a dark place when feeling sleep come over you. There are other aspects of the physical environment that would become uncomfortable for a human. The differences in atmosphere gases would also cause problems on planets easily available to be visited in the physical.

The greatest challenge for a human to visit the home planet of an Earth ET visitor would be the vibration levels of these physical beings. Simply remaining in the presence of too many of them for too long a period would have a detrimental effect upon your mental, then physical function.

This aspect is likely the greatest obstacle to overcome and is not recognized on Earth. Not yet.

Q: *Would we be able to communicate, either in writing or verbally?*
C: Yes, the ET visitors would use a translator and voice sound replicator to create words spoken, and would use it to make you believe they were speaking. Many ET visitors to your Earth have long since physically evolved away from using speech as a form of communication.

Written language would be easy to accomplish, even more simply than verbal communication.

Q: *Why won't the ETs take us to a planet to visit? This assumes humans would be taken to one where physical adaptation would not be difficult.*
C: Beyond entertainment, what purpose would it serve? You who would understand a bit better are not interested in the trip. Many others are wildly keen to do it, but would have their lives changed in what way upon return? The human traveler to an ET planet would be deemed mentally ill if attempting to describe the experience, the sights, sounds, and encounters. The ongoing effect upon such a traveler would be far worse than expected and outweigh the joy of the experience.

Q: *Do they have clouds and storms on some of these planets?*
C: All of the geophysical events and phenomena of Earth occur on ET home worlds, but the broad combinations Earth offers are rare.

Q: *Would humans find gravitational pull a problem?*
C: Yes, on a planet materially larger or smaller than Earth.

Q: *How about wind?*
C: Generally not. The weather patterns on many ET worlds where civilizations have developed to allow long-distance rapid space travel are not threatening. This is except for the occasional storm, just as occurs on Earth.

Q: *Do they have earthquakes and tsunamis?*
C: Yes, these occur.

Q: *How do ETs on the planets travel around?*
C: There are several methods; to travel shorter distances, within the urban centers, there are airborne routes of individual aircraft which flow along much as do vehicles on Earth roadways. To venture farther away, similar and often larger vehicles are used, which can depart the controlled flightways used where congestion is likely.

Q: *Like a combination of aircraft and ground vehicles from Earth?*
C: Yes, this is a good description.

Q: *How about if the distances are very far, such as across or between continents? I'm thinking like one-fifth to half or more of the planet's circumference.*
C: This travel uses methods that shall come to Earth at a point not so far in humanity's future. Balloons are used to rise high above the surface and allow the planet to rotate below. Your Earth revolves in one day; this is faster than any method of propulsion now commonly used.

Q: *How about a Star Trek-like transporter?*
C: This is what your soul does to cross great distance, and the depiction of this procedure in the television program mimics what cannot be done for a physical body, but shows how your energetic being, your soul, moves a great distance.

Q: *What propulsion methods do these aircraft use on the ET worlds? How do they gain lift?*
C: The propulsion is a combination of magnetic and atomic or nuclear energy. The magnetism is used to isolate small clusters of molecules that are then ruptured much as atomic fission has recently been discovered

on Earth. The releasing energy is used for propulsion. Lift is accomplished with antigravity device or gravity cancellation.

Q: *Is the fission done to extract heat energy?*
C: Yes, and the heat is used to create air pressure, which propels the aircraft much as it does with hydrocarbon oxidation or combustion on Earth.

Q: *I imagine these ET "aircars" are very fast.*
C: They can be but are not typically.

Q: *How do they navigate? How do they keep to their "airplanes" and avoid crashes and collisions?*
C: The navigation is achieved with a combination of satellite and ground transmission triangulation. This allows speed, direction, and altitude to be monitored and adjusted automatically. The traveler simply programs the desired destination, and the route is calculated and followed by the aircar's computer.

Q: *What about traffic jams?*
C: These do not occur. Traffic congestion is avoided by expanding, lowering, and lifting air lanes or air conduits as required, automatically. The number of aircars is known, and the master system is permanently monitoring and modifying them to achieve ideal and consistent travel times. The volumes never cause, what you would call, bottlenecks.

Q: *What about parking problems?*
C: These also do not occur; where more visitors than available space for the air vehicles is forecast, the traveler is advised to use surface transit. These are much like your subways and trolleys.

Q: *How do they work?*
C: Electromagnetically and through the elevated, surface, and subsurface tubes.

Q: *Are motorized walkways used?*
C: These are also very common.

Q: *What about a huge gathering in an open area?*
C: The aircars are kept around the perimeter; many of them use small portable hover devices that detach from the vehicle and allow short, one- to two-kilometer travel. Upon arrival, the device will fold into a space no larger than a typical human backpack or large briefcase.

Q: *Are there large buildings?*
C: Of course. These are principally constructed of metal, transparent metals, and silicon compounds similar to or like glass. The external panels are transparent metals, for strength.

Q: *Are there houses, apartment blocks, and similar dwellings?*
C: Yes. Just as on Earth and in greater variety and design. There is generally far more art involved in the design. Much more color.

Q: *How do the ET races generate electricity?*
C: Several methods; one uses planetary magnetism to create pulses, intense light, and photovoltaic panels. What on Earth are your solar panels, using artificially produced light, from the magnetism. Crystals are involved with this method. There is also some use of water flow, also used on Earth. For larger-scale generation, heat energy from nuclear fission is common; however, it is far more efficient and the risk of leaking, radioactive material is eliminated.

Q: *How?*
C: The Earth method initiates a reaction, then controls or dampens it until the nuclear fuel is exhausted. The ability to rupture atoms on a large enough scale to create sufficient heat, on Earth, can only be done with larger, prepared molecules or certain heavy metals. Uranium is Earth's principal material. Uncontrolled, it becomes a dangerous weapon, as was tragically Earth's first use of this method on a larger scale.

Your ET visitor civilizations employ as-needed supplies of simpler compounds where the supply of molecules and the atoms that comprise them can be shut off instantly. This causes the nuclear reaction to halt nearly as quickly. The only risk then becomes inadvertent contact with hot surfaces, a possible problem Earth technology has already solved.

Q: *Do they use water and steam to power a turbine?*
C: Water is not an efficient medium, although it has been used. Ammonia and alcohol-type compounds are used for this, just as humans use them for refrigerants.

Q: *How is food produced?*
C: This wanders into food requirements, which vary widely. Essentially, necessary nutrients are cultivated or manufactured.

Q: *Synthetic food?*
C: Yes.

Q: *What about self-defense? Are there dangerous, predator-like animals?*
C: Yes, there are many species of animals, and, yes, some prey upon others much as the ecological systems on Earth function.

Q: *How is protection from these predators achieved?*
C: Isolation and separation is the preferred method and is part of the development of residential and urban centers. This is done with electromagnetic barriers, which detect and trigger the presence of unwanted intruders.

Q: *What exactly repels the unwanted predator?*
C: There are many methods; sound waves, electrical shocks, and invisible barriers humans would call a force field.

Q: *These do not injure the predator?*
C: No.

Q: *How does the force field work?*
C: It disturbs the bodily electromagnetic signals, disabling the nervous system.

Q: *Temporary paralysis?*
C: Yes.

Q: *How about for explorers or anybody that ventures away from or outside a barrier-protected zone?*
C: These physical beings carry portable devices that achieve similar effects. A crude example would be a stun gun, recently developed on Earth.

Q: *Are these devices lethal?*
C: They can be, if necessary; however, they are rarely used this way on most planets. The objective is safety and to repel an attack.

Q: *OK, we've covered transportation, buildings, electricity, and protection. What about commerce and trade; how are these conducted? What about recycling?*
C: Your question asks also about manufacturing, which you did not cover. Physical goods traded are manufactured in a variety of ways, using some methods Earth dwellers understand, yet done far more efficiently. We refer to chemical production and use. Nearly all materials that can be produced from renewable methods are done this way, and the ability to produce unlimited heat also allows almost complete reuse of materials already produced. Plastics are one example.

Transportation is accomplished by use of both ground and air vehicles. There is no limit to the size and weight of objects that are to be moved. Far less material per person, by weight, is consumed when compared to current Earth dweller use, in the most developed industrial nations of Earth.

Q: *Environmental contamination and pollution?*
C: These have been eliminated.

Q: *Money?*
C: Credit units are common and used exclusively, where employed. There is no physical system of an anonymous medium of exchange, as on Earth.

Q: *I get the impression work and the pursuit of money play a far smaller role in these ET civilizations.*
C: Yes, correct.

Q: *Is barter very common?*
C: Yes, very much so and electronic commerce boards or platforms are used to make goods available and for acquisition with far greater efficiency than humans currently understand.

Q: *What activities are principally pursued, if working in the service of customers is less of the typical activity?*
C: Education, research, and literature are far more common pursuits than Earth dwellers prefer. These activities are seen as entertainment and fun, by the large majority.

Q: *What about crime? Government?*
C: Crime is nearly nonexistent, as a result of telepathic communication. The ability to send and read thoughts before words are produced or processed through sound or sight allow almost all would-be victims of crime to avoid perpetrators. There are very few perpetrations, because the teaching of violence does not work. Because it is nearly futile to be illicit or violent to the detriment of another being or organization, no examples exist to serve as inspiration. So little success with violence occurs that it receives no reinforcement, and does not grow. It nearly never begins.

Government is more mob rule than representative, because of nearly instant understanding, in the collective and individually. There is far less government activity, as any proposal, rule, or procedure a central authority might develop or enforce can be put before the citizens and judges quickly.

Q: *Describe, then, how the societies differ from Earth, in general.*

C: Housing occupies a large portion of human effort to generate perceived wealth to gain use and ownership of a dwelling. In most ET societies, there is far less effort required to produce a dwelling, because transportation is so much more efficient. Available space is abundant, so much more time is available to pursue other interests. Tedium in employment is far less.

Transportation and production of fuels is also a large component of human activity; in the many advanced ET civilizations, there is almost no fuel required and the activity and media of exchange for this are far less common.

Q: *What types of research are pursued?*

C: The galaxy holds so much mystery and intrigue, the available material is unlimited. Humans have no idea, yet, of the vast wonders to be studied and understood.

Q: *Last question: what about disease, sickness, and medical treatment?*

C: Most infectious and chronic diseases have been either eliminated or managed to a point where far less of them occur, and where they do, they are quickly cured, if possible. Sickness is often a simple result of age and deterioration of the physical body, and in many civilizations these conditions develop slowly, as a proportion of the life spans of anyone inflicted are affected. It is not possible to generalize about life spans in terms of human years, as this unit of measurement holds little meaning away from Earth.

Medical treatment is as much preventive as curative, and is less common or necessary. Accidental injury or disease are far higher a proportion of the medical cases that occur, and the overall rate and frequency of required medical treatment conditions is far lower than on Earth among humans.

- 6 -
Physical Appearance

What do ETs look like? They do not look like us. The questions I ask here will be limited to ET visitors to Earth. To ask what beings on other planets resemble is no different from asking what is the appearance of animal life on Earth.

Having never met one myself, I turn to The Committee to inquire about what we might expect to encounter if any of us were either fortunate (*or otherwise*) to meet up with an ET visitor.

Q: *What would we see here on Earth's surface?*
C: We must say, there are among the several dozen ET races visiting and observing Earth from up close, only a handful that would land and make their appearance known generally.

Q: *ET visitors have revealed their physical presence to humans before? Such as to government elected officials?*
C: Yes, but not very many elected officials themselves. This has become rare in the age of self-protection, the age when portable, lethal methods of self-defense are employed when the risk of attackers using these same implements and techniques has also become feasible.

It is very risky for the calm encounter, that an extraterrestrial would appear before a head of state without provoking a rapid and immediate response from nearby security agents. Bear in mind, always, that tight screening and analysis does not prevent the risk that staff, employees, and visitors considered otherwise safe will not misbehave or directly threaten the subject of the security forces.

This means the protected person, what you might name the protectee, also has methods and procedures to call protection for defense. Such agents would likely harm the extraterrestrial, who understands this very well.

Q: *If the influential elected officials are not contacted, who is? In government?*

C: Military and security agents themselves.

Q: *Since the chapter deals with appearance, I'll stick to that. What reactions did the ETs get?*
C: The expected. The ETs anticipated this and took steps to protect themselves and calm their temporary hosts.

Q: *What steps?*
C: Disable the visited people from acting against them.

Q: *I imagined it worked.*
C: Of course. However, the visited humans did not react badly, because they understood immediately they were not under attack. Many have not attempted to repel the visitors.

Q: *What do ETs look like physically? Do they wear clothing?*
C: Yes, they wear garments just as do humans, in many, many cases. Where climate and temperature allow clothing to be optional, it is not so rare for extraterrestrials to not use cloth coverings for their bodies; however, they know humans would react less positively. In the majority of cases, garments are used normally, so this is no different.

Q: *How many races have visited Earth and made contact with humans, recently? I mean over the last century?*
C: Overall, five.

Q: *How did each appear? Tall, short, what color, what shape bodies, limbs, digits, and so forth?*
C: There are variations of height just as with humans, so this answer is not easy to provide. We can say the average physical height, among the visitors and presenters of themselves on Earth, is taller than the average human.

Q: *What color are they?*
C: The predominant skin tone or color is gray, although there are variations. The silicon chemical basis for their biochemical composition is not red in the circulatory system, of the visitors seen on Earth. This is part of the human appearance, although skin of humans is colored by materials or substances that protect against sun, independent of the chemical makeup of blood. As you know, there are many humans who look almost grayish.

The ETs also look grayish yet the redness of skin seen in the human face caused by blood flow does not occur in ETs with silicon-based chemistries.

Q: *Do they have body or head hair?*
C: No.

Q: *What is the average height? Do they have genders?*
C: Yes, there are genders; few are androgynous. This does exist in some races. The average height is what humans would measure as two meters. There are examples of two and half meters and taller.

Q: *Fingers and toes?*
C: Yes, as well developed as in humans. There is increased dexterity and strength in the manual digits, and a natural ability to do more than balance the foot, with the podiatric digits.

Q: *They can run and jump?*
C: Yes, and better than most humans.

Q: *How large are their heads?*
C: This varies and again we answer with respect to the visitor races having intentionally made themselves appear. The head or cranium enclosure, the skull bone you would call it, is approximately 30 percent more capacious than the average human.

Q: *What about their eyes and mouth?*
C: There are two eyes and these are darker than what humans typically have, and there is little white eyeball material visible. The eyes are more than twice the size of typical human eye organs, among the ET visitors Earth has received. The opening for light to enter and reach the retina is both larger and can close itself almost completely. In some cases, the cornea, which opens and closes to increase or reduce light entering, is vertical. It resembles the eye opening of some animals on Earth, however is not horizontal. These characteristics provide a double protection against bright light and allow the exposure to bright light without diminishing the visible image as much.

Q: *So they don't have to squint?*
C: No, the eyelids are more for physical protection than light reduction.

Q: *Do they have ears?*
C: Yes, two external ones, also larger in relation to the outer, external ear than is the average human ear to the human head. They are able to turn the ear almost as might an animal on Earth, in some cases.

Q: *Are we humans going to see these traits and characteristics in all extraterrestrial visitors that have and will visit Earth?*
C: No, we are describing what is seen in several. There will be variations.

Q: *How about head hair?*
C: Some yes, some no.

Q: *Body hair?*
C: Not common, and this will not be encountered with ET visitors to Earth. What little there will be found is nearly invisible.

Q: *Knees, elbows, jawbones, teeth, and so forth?*
C: Yes, the limbs are jointed and also at the location of the joining of the human wrist and foot.

Q: *How good are ETs' eyesight, hearing, and smell?*
C: All of these sensory perceptions are more sensitive and better developed in ability than common to a human. The ET visitors Earth will briefly and rarely get, can see in darker conditions as well as animals of Earth, or even better. They can pick up a far broader range of sound frequency, much as Earth animals do and have the olfactory ability of many untamed animals of Earth.

Q: *How physically strong are they, how fast can they run, and do they have any special abilities not immediately apparent?*
C: There is greater endurance and stamina than the appearance would suggest; however, Earth's atmosphere has an effect on some, to a degree. This is not large and would not debilitate any of them. If risk of becoming weak or otherwise temporarily disabled were a strong possibility, such races or members of them would not expose themselves.

They are stronger per unit of weight than are humans, when comparing beings from similar planetary gravity effects. Some will find Earth's lower gravity to be a significant strength enhancer, others will find Earth's gravity similar. None who visit your Earth surface who shall have contact with or around humans comes from a planet where smaller size and lesser gravity will make Earth's gravity field a burden.

Q: *If attacked or threatened, how would they defend themselves?*
C: They would use a three-tiered method. First, they would mentally disable an attacker by disturbing the operation of the brain. Some have the mental energy ability to do this to a human. They cannot do it to one another with much success yet have the ability to do so to a human. This aspect is no different from many things in the Earth environment. The ability to use arms to work can also be used negatively, and in fact human weapons are called arms for this reason. As you all know.

So the telepathic ability can be turned against a human negatively, if required.

Q: *Would this cause discomfort, pain, or injury?*
C: No.

Q: *It would not be like Darth Vader in* Star Wars, *where he suddenly uses mental power to cause someone to choke, collapse, and suffocate to death?*
C: No, although this possibility exists.

Q: *How likely is it to be misused?*
C: Zero. No use of this ability would occur unless forced by host provocations or threats.

Q: *What would be the second tier or method?*
C: They could physically restrain or contain a human threat.

Q: *By themselves or with implements like handcuffs?*
C: No, they are well versed in what would be called martial arts and other methods and techniques of exercise, defense, and agility. They could easily use any human physical attack's force against the would-be foe. This is in the case of small numbers of attackers and ET targets.

Q: *What about a larger attack, say twenty or thirty humans against two visitors? Like a mob of people against just two arriving ET ship crew members?*
C: The mental ability to disable brain operation works by proximity, not size of group. Human brain waves and patterns are well studied and understood by your ET cousins. They know how to neutralize human brainwave activity to the point the human is suspended from attacking them.

Q: *Would the ET leave a human tied up or otherwise restrained?*
C: Yes, until they departed the scene and no risk of injury remains.

Q: *How would they release the bindings?*
C: A simple electronic timer. It would use unknown units of measurement and offer a clue into the planetary starlight thus time measurement used by the ET, but would not have much significance to human understanding or technology.

Q: *OK, what then would the ETs use as the third tier or level of defense?*
C: Physical weapons.

Q: *What are these?*
C: Electromagnetic stun devices. They can either temporarily disable or kill a target. No ET visitor would use such device unless forced to do

so, to protect its own physical well-being, and would never kill a human until all possibilities of ending the conflict without injury or death have been pursued.

Q: *What's the risk they would kill or injure a human?*
C: Nearly zero. The other methods would be very effective.

Q: *We are getting into the material of the next chapter, so I will just ask one more thing about ET physical appearance. Will the overall appearance frighten people?*
C: Yes, in general. To lessen this, the ETs have provided images of themselves and described what they would do when meeting, lending deep credibility to the contact by repeating to their visited hosts details such hosts are certain no outsider could know.

This both alarms and calms the first time contacted, who understand no foe could or would take such steps. No known foe has the capability. It is impossible to know at the time of the image contact, if there will be appearing a being of such traits, yet when it occurs, the remaining accurate but very confidential information will now be understood to have been obtained by the same being whose image was already supplied.

This calms the visited one, who understands the futility of denial, defensive attack, preemptive strike, or flight from the area. None of these would have effect.

- 7 -
Technologies

Technology means devices, methods, and mechanical operations ET visitors both have and use. Some are not necessarily used near or on Earth. I don't ask about those, but I think some of that bleeds through anyway. Nevertheless, why should we know or care what ETs do away from Earth, even if we do? For the time being, anyway.

We do not yet have the technologies on Earth but are likely to develop along the course of Earth history.

To assist, I ask The Committee to speak generally about all of the ET civilizations that have come to Earth and do so now; which come into Earth's orbit and sometimes send a scout ship into the atmosphere, physically land on the surface and in a few cases, make contact with humans. Not every civilization does all of these things. There are ET civilizations that observe Earth from a great distance, by what we understand to be great distances on or relative to Earth. These other ET civilizations do not come into our solar system.

OBSERVATION

Q: *Let's start with that last part of the previous paragraph; do the*
      observer ET civilizations, which do not come to our solar
      system, have many of the technologies actual visitors also
      possess?
C: Yes; there are many overlaps among them.

Q: *How do long-distance observers watch Earth? Through a telescope?*
C: Yes, a type of telescope yet the device does not operate with light
      photons limited to the speed of light Earth human dimensions believe to
      be the ultimate limit.

Q: *Can you please explain?*
C: Just as there are colors and types of light humans cannot see, or sounds
      humans cannot hear that have been proved to exist, with causes and

effects able to be heard by other animals on Earth as an example, are there also variations of light humans likewise do not and cannot detect.

The light photons humans observe are limited to the velocity of the electron movement that creates the electromagnetic pulses and light.

The energy that makes electrons orbit the nucleus of an atom is not limited to the speed or velocity of the bumping or jumping of atoms between molecules. Electricity is not simply a flow of electrons; it is the mass, collective simultaneous movement of many electrons from one atom to the next or nearby atom.

The energy that both holds an electron in orbit and causes it to revolve, is not limited to 300,000 kilometers per second, in Earth units of distance and time.

This energy permeates all matter, is connected to all things, and moves at velocities that are truly instantaneous.

This means light generates several images, similar and uniform, which can be observed at different levels of vibrations or within different vibrational frequencies.

Q: *That was a head full of information! So, let's see if I understood correctly; light happens and creates several simultaneous images. Each one can be observed at the same instant by different receivers or observers, depending on the frequency of the image and the frequency to which the receiver tunes in.*

C: That is essentially correct; however, we will adjust your interpretation and say, not the frequency of the image but rather the frequency the receiver allows. All light, energy, and electromagnetic transmissions, emissions, and creations contain all of the possible frequency ranges. There is not a process to tune the output sent; this part is automatic.

It is the ability to receive, or to tune in to the energy, to observe it.

Q: *So light takes several minutes to travel from the sun to the Earth ...*
C: ... on Earth, from the Earth human point-of-view. The light humans can see.

Q: *It's possible to speed ahead of the light we can see or maybe see it twice?*
C: Yes. As many times as the human vibration limit allows. If, from the human level, one Earth minute of viewing the sun is to be observed fifteen times, this will be impossible. The Earth time environment and speed of light does not allow fifteen minutes for light to reach Earth

from your sun, which requires less. If the image originating on the sun is to be observed five, rather than fifteen times, this is simple and can be achieved, since the light requires more than five minutes.

Q: *This means the observer has to slow down and speed up, say five times as in your example, to catch, overtake, then stop to observe. Correct?*
C: Yes, easily done.

Q: *How fast does the light move?*
C: The light energy is instantaneous; it is slower for and within the human occupied vibrational range.

Q: *It sounds as if the range is intended for humans, to limit us.*
C: No, not even close. These ranges have always existed and are mathematical functions of one another. This will become understood as the higher frequency ranges are demonstrated.

Q: *Do the light images diminish in strength and intensity over distance, just as happens with humans?*
C: Yes, but no. The diminished ability is caused by human limitations to visual acuity, overcome with magnification. Just as microscopes enlarge what is otherwise too small for the human eye to see, so do the observer telescopes enlarge the image observed from many parsecs, to use a human measure of distance.

Q: *Is this anything like the electron microscope humans use to see very small things?*
C: Yes! The principles are the same, the telescopes used by your ET cousins are essentially microscopes that observe the energy stream that controls electrons.

Q: *ET observers point their telescopes at Earth, zoom in, and watch what we do?*
C: They listen also.

Q: *ET visitors to Earth can do this from orbit?*
C: As easily as you can look at your hand.

Q: *Are ETs able to observe or look through what we consider to be solid objects? In other words, they can make walls invisible?*
C: Yes, the image observed can be separated from the energy signature of the solid object that otherwise obscures it.

Q: *How?*
C: All matter has an energy pattern, what could be called an energy

signature. The Earth dimensions allow one to block another, by proximity. The energy behind the light humans observe, which causes the object farther way to be equally observable, does not encounter the limitation in higher vibrational ranges.

Q: *Is this why spirits and souls, as energetic beings, can pass through what some think are solid objects?*

C: Yes, precisely. Because the higher vibrational ranges allow the limitations of physicality to be removed, so do they remove the limits of observance or sight.

Q: *ETs on a planet halfway across the galaxy can observe us just as things are occurring on Earth, at the same time?*

C: Yes. Increasing distances affect magnification. Not all ET civilizations observing Earth have the same magnification ability.

PROPULSION

Q: *What about propulsion? How do ETs move their spacecraft? What energy do they use to maneuver or propel them across the great distances?*

C: To assume the distances are great is also a function of Earth time and light speed limits. Lift the illusion of Earth time, which does not apply away from your planet, and the idea a distance is large fades away.

Q: *I am certain you're going to say, the limits of light's speed are also an illusion that makes distance seem vast.*

C: This we will not say, for you have just said it for us.

Q: *A nearby star is said to be, say, ten light years distant. Two decades would be the round trip to visit planets there.*

C: If travel were undertaken with propulsion technology Earth residents now understand, yes.

Q: *How long does an ET visitor require to make the round trip to visit Earth?*

C: In Earth time, this is done in approximately three to four hours, to make the circuit.

Q: *Is it faster or slower depending on where the planet is, where the trip is begun?*

C: No and yes. The location does affect the travel span, yet linear distance does not. A planet farther from Earth in a straight line can be reached faster than one closer in a straight line, in some cases.

Q: *How is this accomplished?*
C: Space compression. The notion of distance travel on Earth requires
     the distance to be fixed, because the environment, in which the origin
     and destination are located, is fixed relative to the traveler. Once outside
     the solid matter environment of a planet, this fixation does not apply.

     The Earth's gaseous atmosphere cannot be compressed without
     negative effects; damage and death are two outcomes of this, and travel
     through this gas encounters a fixed resistance. A steady force against
     which propulsion must act. The destinations of Earth human travel
     always involve a destination upon the hard planet surface. Also factored
     in to the equation are Earth gravity and magnetism, as this involves
     objects in close orbit.

     Travel between planets only encounters plasma, charged electrons,
     and ions as the cause of resistance. There are very few of these relative
     to the environment of a planet. The density and occurrence are far
     lower. There are almost infinitesimally fewer ions in outer space. The
     electrons stripped from atoms in a cloud become lightning; this cannot
     occur in space, as there are not enough and no destination atoms for the
     electrons to attach.

     In this environment, unlike upon or near Earth, both interplanetary
     interstellar forces and physical resistance are not present. This allows
     compression.

Q: *How is this done?*
C: The interstellar traveler twists or warps the proportions a straight line
     represents, by following a circular route or in practice, many of them.

Q: *The traveler ship bends space?*
C: Compresses it, but the effect is the same. The key is to compress it
     along the infinite number of circles, globes really, which exist between
     and among all things. To draw the far edge of the circle closer, to
     tighten the loop. This is achieved by jumping from one curved segment,
     or arc, to another.

Q: *How is this done?*
C: Once the resistance of Earth travel is understood to be absent, the ends
     of the arc are brought together with acceleration. This is achieved with
     magnetic amplification, employing crystals. The resulting energy is
     tuned or aligned to match the resonant frequency of the destination.
     This has a two-staged effect, to compress then expand. The
     compression is the first half of the trip, the expansion or relaxation of
     the compression achieves the second half of the movement.

These follow the curved lines of the globes along which all magnetic energy follows, as all of you know from tracking the magnetic flux lines of any magnet on Earth.

Q: *Does this require a lot of power?*
C: No, the requirement is proportional to the size of the vessel, not the perceived distance. Once the levels of power match the mass of the ship, then tuning of the amplified frequency to the destination signature is all that is required.

Q: *So a vessel doing this can cross the galaxy in one or two hours?*
C: Yes, of Earth time.

Q: *And it is magnetic attraction that does this?*
C: Yes.

PROTECTION AND DEFENSE

Q: *I have channeled before that ET scout ships disabled weapons systems of approaching Earth aircraft that attempted to fire on them.*
C: Yes.

Q: *How was this done?*
C: Electromagnetic energy; as the approaching aircraft readied its weapons to fire, the systems and aircraft itself were disabled with intense, directed electromagnetic energy. It is generated with controlled nuclear fission, the rupture of the several atoms being used to provide the energy.

Q: *How was it aimed at the aircraft?*
C: The fission reactor has controlled openings, which are pointed in the direction of the target. There are many heavy metals which block and absorb intense electromagnetic energy. Iron and lead serve this purpose on Earth, yet there are metals not present on Earth that achieve the same effect.

The several million atoms are separated and then ruptured inside the chamber, which nearly instantly create an intense energy field or pulse. As this is done, the electromagnetic energy is allowed to escape for a few brief microseconds, which floods the nearby space with enough to disable and render electronic circuitry useless.

Q: *How are the ET scout ships able to know an Earth aircraft will fire upon them?*

C: Simple; they both monitor the aircraft-to-ground communications and the pilot's own thoughts.

Q: *Would this electromagnetic pulse damage or injure the pilot?*
C: No, not for a brief moment. Prolonged exposure might do such a thing, yet a brief intense burst would not. There are insufficient materials in the human body to catch or otherwise be affected by such energy.

Q: *Can this technology be used on the ground to disable any weapon?*
C: Yes, with alterations. To prevent the use of a firearm, the would-be target reads the intent and desire of a shooter and neutralizes the shooter's nervous system. Much the way this would be done with what on Earth is called a stun gun, which is a crude and unrefined method. The ET visitor has the ability to direct electrical interference to the limb or limbs which would be used to initiate an attack.

Q: *Can the explosion of gunpowder be stopped?*
C: No, not once begun. The ability to neutralize a weapon that does not require electricity to operate is less effective with ET technology. In this case, the ET would physically remove the weapon from the grip or proximity of its human user with an electrical discharge similar to what would be called lightning. This risks injury to the shooter, so avoidance of the violent encounter is the preferred method.

Q: *How did ET visitors protect themselves when meeting with humans who were surrounded by security, many of them armed with guns?*
C: By telling them what would happen and demonstrating the ability to kill all humans present, with no ability of the humans to prevent it. To make the humans understand that if the ET visitors had ill intent, they would have already used it.

This is similar to a human adult in the presence of a baby, where no ability exists for the infant to halt an attack, lethal or otherwise, which the adult might carry out.

Unlike human babies, human visitors understand immediately they need fear nothing.

***

This leads us to the next technology ...

COMMUNICATION

Q: *How do the ETs communicate with humans if they generally do not use speech?*

C: The ETs use a translator to convert their thoughts to words, which appear either spoken artificially or written, as the circumstances require.

Q: *The ETs use an electronic speech generator?*

C: Yes. These are programmed to reproduce all human spoken and written languages, and are compact enough to fit inside the mouth of an ET to provide the illusion of speech.

Q: *Do ETs have vocal chords?*

C: Yes, but these would more correctly be called sound chords, because ETs do not use them to formulate speech with the larynx, tongue, mouth, and teeth. Simply to make general sounds.

Q: *Can they understand human speech?*

C: Yes, but they hear the speech, and already understand the thoughts which precede then result in speech, which follows the thoughts. As a person speaking begins to talk, the complete idea is generally already formed. The sentence becomes redundant, but for the other humans who might require hearing it. The ETs know this.

Q: *How about written speech?*

C: ETs can read any human language put before them.

Q: *How about long-distance communication? For example, how far away do ETs need to be, to no longer be able to see us on the Earth's surface?*

C: Approximately one-quarter the distance across the galaxy.

Q: *That far?*

C: This distance is not so far, consider the distances between galaxies.

Q: *How about audio communication? Is this able to be done by ETs over a farther distance?*

C: Unlike Earth, no. Visual images and audio sound can both be transmitted across similar distances, the difference is transmitter and receiver capacity. The limits and abilities of these devices used by ETs exceeds the requirement for such communication.

Q: *It is possible to send a visual image as far as a voice message?*

C: Yes, assuming there is an optical capture device, what Earth beings call a camera, to create a digital file of the image.

Q: *Does this apply to still images or moving?*
C: Moving images are simply a series of still images and device capacity
       is what limits them, as we have said, the capacity well exceeds the need
       to send images.

Q: *I assume these signals move at the same speeds as the ability to travel?*
C: Faster, essentially instantly, across the galaxy.

Q: *What energy sources do these devices use, electricity? If so, how do
       they generate it?*
C: Yes, electricity is used and it is generated several ways, none currently
       used on Earth, although this will change.

POWER

Q: *Can you describe these methods?*
C: One method uses existing magnetism to generate a small current, and
       the source is the natural magnetic field of a planet. The current is
       stored, built up like a battery charge, then used to create a pulse or
       spark of electricity. This spark is amplified through a crystal to produce
       a brilliant burst of light, which is converted into electricity chemically,
       by means of photovoltaic cells. What humans call solar panels.

       Another method used, where no natural magnetic field is present, is
       nuclear fission. On Earth, the use of this method is to produce heat
       energy. The Earth use is still crude and requires a large amount of
       material, and was first employed in a runaway reaction, or explosive
       weapon. A bomb.

       Later, the reaction was controlled yet remains large. The risk of it
       running away remains.

       The method used away from Earth by ET civilizations controls fission,
       or the sequential rupture of atoms, by controlling the amount of
       material used to create the fission and release of magnetic and heat
       energy. There are several methods that take advantage of both.

       In place of water, different chemicals and liquid metals, such as
       mercury, are used to transfer the heat energy into rotating motion. The
       magnetic pulse the fission produces can also be stored in a battery,
       after passing through a coil mounted for this precise purpose. The
       battery storage of the electricity is much more long lasting than Earth

technology currently employs, and the decay or run down of the battery charge is almost nonexistent.

Q: *How is the battery kept from running down?*
C: It is isolated so the energy finds no ground or place to flow.

Q: *How is the magnetic medium isolated?*
C: Vacuum suspension.

Q: *How does the small nuclear reaction not "run away"?"*
C: It runs away; however, the amount of atomic material or fuel is controlled. Once the molecules and atoms of the material have been ruptured nearly completely, another dose is injected into the fission chamber and the process begun again.

Q: *Like fuel injection in a gasoline or diesel engine?*
C: Conceptually similar, yes.

Q: *How does this happen? Enormous pressure is required to initiate nuclear fission.*
C: Electricity or, specifically, what you call electromotive potential on Earth, is used to accelerate the material at high enough velocity over sufficient distance that the effect is similar.

Q: *We use atom smashers that are several kilometers long to break up just one atom!*
C: Sufficient velocity shortens the distance to approximately one meter of your Earth units.

Q: *How can this be done?*
C: The fissile material is charged and the surrounding field of plasma is charged oppositely, to an electromotive potential sufficiently powerful to pull or draw the atoms of the fissile material into one another to smash one and begin the reaction.

Q: *What is the fissile material?*
C: Liquid metal. Mercury is one Earth example that remains in the liquid state at normal ambient Earth temperatures, yet others can be melted at easily achieved temperatures, such as two or three thousand degrees centigrade, then injected.

Q: *Are the surrounding components made of ceramics?*
C: Yes, similar type materials, unaffected by the temperatures used to liquefy the fissile material or fuel, or the fission reaction itself.

Q: How do the ETs start this device up, when it's cold and turned off?
C: Stored battery power.

Q: Are these devices reliable?
C: Completely.

Q: If we visit an ET planet, we'd discover what methods for generating electricity?
C: Variations of the above, in less compact form. There are no combustion methods used that produce potentially harmful emissions, and water flow is rarely used. This method is ideal but for the limits to transmission over distance. In some cases, it will be discovered that ET civilizations have built urban centers close to hydrologic sources to minimize transmission loss of power; however, other planets simply use magnetic potential, which is equally available everywhere.

NAVIGATION AND MANEUVERABILITY

Q: Once the ET "mother ship" reaches Earth, I assume it does not enter Earth's atmosphere, correct?
C: Rarely; however, this has been done.

Q: These vessels are large by human standard?
C: Yes, some of them.

Q: How does the scout ship propel itself, and how does it stay airborne? Can and do they land on the surface?
C: The small ship uses magnetic differential for propulsion, although it has backup thermal capability. The backup is the previously mentioned nuclear fission. In those cases, the heat generated is no different from heat energy generated by combustion of your hydrocarbon compounds with oxygen. The rapid oxidation.

Q: How does a scout ship use magnetism?
C: Earth is a massive magnet, as are many planets. The smaller vessels simply create measured, opposite, and also similar polarity charges against the fixed and predictable Earth field. As your science has understood very well, like polarities repel, opposite poles attract. The size of Earth's magnetic field is far more than sufficient to move almost any size vessel easily, or to suspend it, through use of like and opposite polarities.

Q: *Does the mother ship also use this method to remain above Earth?*

C: It can and sometimes they do; however, not always. In some cases, the ship simply allows orbit to be achieved through gravity, much as humans have already learned to do.

Q: *Why can't we see the mother ship?*

C: It is cloaked, both from view and from radar. Many of you have looked directly at one and not seen it.

Radar signals are radio transmissions reflected back; this is easy to defeat. The cloaked ship simply emits a reverse phase signal and cancels the arriving signal and reflection. No return signal is produced and nothing returns to the radar transceiver.

Q: *How can the large ship—or even the small scout ships—know what signal is being aimed at them?*

C: The signals are never aimed, because the presence of the target is unknown. The general radar signal is broadcast over a large area. It moves at the speed of light and electricity and is thus easy to anticipate. A far higher velocity version or imprint of this signal emanates simultaneously. It is detected and used to replicate then reverse its effects.

Q: *Like sound or noise cancellation?*

C: Precisely.

Q: *How are we prevented from seeing the ships?*

C: The exterior is covered with light emitting devices similar to diodes; however, the technology of chemistry is different. These emit an image that matches the background against which the ship might be seen, so looking directly at a cloaked device reveals nothing.

Q: *What about the cases where we indeed do see an ET scout ship in the atmosphere?*

C: These are intentional.

Q: *Why do the ETs want to be seen?*

C: So you know they exist.

Q: *Can the ET ships land?*

C: Of course, and have.

Q: *Why do they fly close to Earth? If they can observe almost anything from orbit, what's the point?*

C: Do you enjoy live observation or a video feed of it? The same curiosity humans have, exists everywhere. It is always a unique experience to observe a sporting event in person with your eyes, when compared to a television broadcast of it.

Q: *Esteemed Committee, thank you for this information.*
C: Our pleasure.

- 8 -
History of ETs on Earth

The history of extraterrestrial presence on Earth is really the story about Earth history and human presence on it. Before there were humans, there were ETs; they created us. Chapter 1 describes the process of humanoid introduction and what evolved into the human beings we are today, what we have been for dozens of millennia.

The involvement with human civilization has been more active in previous civilizations and has dwindled to almost nothing over the last two dozen centuries, give or take.

The involvement has largely been observation of humanity and also human observation of visitors. Many symbols and depictions are to be found in statues and carvings human civilizations have left behind, and the visitors have left many things for us to examine.

The statues on Easter Island in the Pacific Ocean were built by extraterrestrial visitors, and have since sunk partially into and have been surrounded by the soil upon which they once stood proudly. These statues are a good representation of the physical form, but not the color, of the visitors who left them behind. The location was selected for its remoteness and human inability to reach it, while the ETs used this place as a base from which to explore the Earth.

Stonehenge in England is also an example of visitor presence, and was placed there as a marker. The stone was removed and cut from Earth rock far from the location and transported using gravity neutralization; no surface vehicles were required. Stonehenge sits atop a node or connection point of many flux lines part of Earth's gravity field, which is the reason the location was chosen. The magnetic signature of this spot made for a good homing beacon; it gave travelers an easy and quick way to reach the surface in this part of the world.

The pyramids of Egypt, the initial trio long since stripped of their polished stone cap or surface, were also constructed by extraterrestrial visitors, for similar reason and purpose.

The South American nation of Peru also contains its share of ET-built and -influenced structures, many considered to originate with the indigenous people discovered by Spanish explorers in the sixteenth century. It is true that the structures, upon many of which the Spaniards constructed their own buildings, such as churches, "belonged" to the indigenous civilizations; however, these were not designed or constructed by them. ETs did this long before the local civilizations populated those places. The massive size of the stones and their amazingly precise fit, the gap into which not even a sheet of paper can be inserted, were not possible with the technology—or lack of it—possessed by the Inca. Many subsequent seismic events have caused the Spanish structures to crumble, whereas the ET-built "foundations" have not been disturbed even slightly. The design, assembly, and durability of these edifications are clear evidence that something advanced far beyond Earth civilizations designed, cut, levitated, and assembled what is found today.

Strong evidence of ET influence is also found all around the world; the amazingly precise Aztec Calendar Stone, indeed carved by the human civilization, was influenced by both ET visitor and the guardian guides of its creators. The arrangement and design of the Mexican Pyramids were also influenced by visitors, although the construction was done by humans who fled and escaped the destruction of Atlantis.

Many of Egypt's later structures, such as the Sphinx and the adjacent, smaller but less precise pyramids, were done by the Atlantis escapees. The entire civilization of what became Egypt was stimulated and influenced by the ET visitors, whose presence diminished and was eventually forgotten.

Humans have discovered the preservation effects of pyramids, an effect long and well understood by ETs. The burial of Egyptian pharaohs within the chambers precisely located for preservation effect was done with this knowledge, although the chambers were not built for burial. They were created during design and construction to house ET power sources, transmissions from which enhanced the image of the pyramids from far in outer space. Pharaohs' tombs came well after this period was over, the equipment long since removed.

The most obvious recent evidence of ETs on Earth is made up of the continuous and ever so interesting crop circles. These temporary bits of good-natured graffiti are done when crops have grown to the point of near harvest, where output will not be materially affected. Rarely if ever discussed, is why the crop formations always appear in well-grown, nearly mature crops; the formations and shapes never appear in newly planted fields, although they could, and when viewed from the altitude of small aircraft, draw precise, straight, and curved lines impossible to be done from the surface without sophisticated equipment.

These are always done near populated areas where overhead aircraft are virtually certain to discover them immediately; they are not visible from the ground and appear to a person on the surface to be simply trampled or broken crops, the work of vandalism or mischief and nothing more.

Closer inspection reveals precise bending of the crop stems, with no damage to them in any other fashion. In some cases, the crops continue to live. No pattern of human footprints, equipment, vehicle tracks, debris, residue, or other evidence of human presence has ever been detected.

Speculative explanations never progress beyond vague theories; no credible explanation has been offered how these appear in the morning when the very afternoon before there was no hint of the formation, often fifty to one hundred meters in size. The idea humans could do this using wooden boards and ropes at night never explains how this would be accomplished in the dark. No sign of lights has ever been detected in the fields where these crop formations occur.

Residual magnetism is common when the sites are inspected shortly afterward, another anomaly that defies explanation.

The many crop formations and circular depictions have been interpreted as riddles; indeed, in many, many cases, precise celestial and scientific information is represented by the shapes and formations within them.

How are they done?

The technologies explained in chapter 7 are used to conceal the presence of the scout ship; it simply descends to the chosen location and uses an electromagnetic beam focused to the exact height and location required to bend the shaft of the growing plant along the lines of the figure being drawn. Much the way we use machines to make repeat passes over the surface of material to be engraved, using a grid overlay to fix coordinates and precise points, do the ETs choose four points to represent the corners of the figure or image they draw. They simply make as many repeated passes over the surface of the image as needed. In only a few minutes, the work is done and they depart. In silence and complete invisibility, they quickly leave their drawing and riddled message for us to decipher, to their subsequent delight and joy.

- 9 -
Purposes

This will be a short chapter on an important subject, possibly the most relevant of the book. What objective do ETs have for visiting Earth? Couldn't they just ignore Earth or, as we know from responses to questions in previous chapters, completely conceal their presence?

Yes, certainly they could and on this subject, the author is being strongly prompted—urged is probably a better word—to transcribe the thoughts from one such civilization tuned into the writing of this book as it's being done.

I do not get strong visuals of ETs, and often no visuals of many things about which answers come to questions, either mine or from readers of material I produce. In this case, the same applies; I am not getting a mental image to match the message offered, so I cannot say what's coming through is like a transcript of a face-to-face interview. The message, however, is strong and to the point.

I turn the microphone over to the extraterrestrial beings who strongly wish to speak to the readership and humanity about their reasons for disclosing their presence and the purposes they have in establishing contact with Earth.

They say:

"Greetings and salutations, in the ways and words you prefer visitors offer them, and allow us to expand on this important question.

"Our purpose is to lift you. There is no greater purpose or goal we hope to reach. We have been graciously and often, magnanimously, contacted, by what we once considered to be alien civilizations unknown on our planets. We say planets, because we speak for and on behalf of many civilizations interested in Earth, its societies, and its future.

"We are what you might call an advisory board or panel of consultants, in the absence of a more accurate term, interested in assisting the growth, well-being, and beneficent development of humanity and its happiness.

"We say we are similar to a board or panel but are not like one, where such group of advisers have been formed at either the request of, or invitation from, members of the organization to be counseled. There is no human group of representatives which have sought to form us into a body of thought, a group that would offer our knowledge at the behest of the humans who might receive it. So, we are not a panel, board, committee, or group as you might understand we could be.

"This partially explains our reluctance to appear and inadvertently interfere with mankind, although we know this would not be inadvertent. We know our more direct and open contact would amount to an intrusion and result in distortion and interference to some degree.

"The effects might be welcomed and even embraced by the some of you, yet not by all and certainly, not a majority. The net effects of the combined reactions would come to be the interfering intrusion we hope to avoid.

"We are interested in preparation for the time the agreement expires, when more open and direct contact is again permitted. Long ago, when the first humanoids were created on Earth, the observer civilizations came together and agreed there would be limited and, eventually, very restrictive contact with Earth. The early contacts were made to help us understand Earth, its environment, and the several courses of development humanity might follow.

"The choices to develop individually, and also to create societies, have been made solely by the humans, in their souls before incarnation and while on Earth, living the life agreements each soul has made with itself and its fellow souls, who might also accompany one another.

"As human development advanced, contact with civilizations from other planets has reduced. Humans have also moved away from a spiritual belief that more easily accepted many aspects of human existence than is common now. At one time, it was common to accept the existence of one's soul, and others who did not understand these aspects were simply considered to be unfamiliar with the concepts.

"With the spread of organized religion, the idea that souls exist, endure, and that there are civilizations from other planets, has fallen from favor. The rise in scientific knowledge has contributed to more closure in many ways. The requirement for scientific proof has fed this change.

"Just as humans are intensely interested in all aspects of biology, physiology, and the behavior of living things on Earth, so are all civilizations throughout the galaxy and universe.

"To observe and understand are the reasons for our interest, our purpose to help lift humanity in the ways it chooses to rise. To gain knowledge, understanding, and growth.

"These gifts were given to our civilizations by many generous visitors to our worlds, and we feel a natural urge and obligation to pass them along.

"Never shall we interfere, never shall we distort. All decisions must be followed according to the choices of humanity. To provide knowledge and understanding of the likely outcomes are the most we can hope to do.

"Slowly and in measured, careful steps do we reveal certain things about our existence and knowledge, especially through humanity's atomic age. This development has thrust the challenges of nuclear physics upon mankind, and it is our obligation to ensure the greater benefit ensues from its development.

"When the days of more contact come, and this book forms part of the preemptive contact which precedes those days, we shall bask in the pride we have for you. It is our objective to do this, and to welcome you all to our family openly. You have always been a part of us and now, in a greater way, shall the many humans know of their place, history, and role in the galaxy and universe. So immense is our pride, so deep our gratitude to others who did this for us, that we eagerly seek yet patiently await the time when we are given the honor of doing so, for mankind upon Earth.

"Farewell and always."

- 10 -
What Do They Want Here?

Of the billions of stars and many billions more planets orbiting them in just our galaxy alone, it is logical to wonder what attraction Earth offered that drew extraterrestrial visitor attention. There are so many planets to examine, Earth could easily get lost in such a large number. We're only one marble in a barrel of them, the size of an oil storage tank.

The gold-mining expeditions that resulted in the creation of humanoids don't explain the recurring visits, certainly not five hundred centuries' worth.

Did extraterrestrial visitors come to Earth before the gold miners came?

"Yes," says The Committee, "the humanoid creators were not the first visitors to Earth from other civilizations. Earth had been orbited and its surface visited many times before. Some of these visits were quick observations of the life and conditions, others were more extensive and intended to study the biochemistry."

What made the gold miners stay?

"Unlike previous explorers, the miner ETs were specifically looking for gold to be used for their own purposes, and knew it could be found on planets of similar composition to ones where gold had already been located.

"The attraction of large amounts of gold on Earth is what caused the decision to stay and extract it. It is ground into small enough dust particles so that once cast into the middle and upper atmospheres of many planets, the gold dust will have a beneficial effect on climate and weather; the presence of the gold will make weather patterns more steady, more predictable, and will eliminate weather extremes, including storms, droughts, or excessive precipitation."

We must now ask, how much gold was taken away?

"Nearly all of it," responds The Committee, "and of the remaining gold now on Earth, we say it is less than 10 percent of the original amount. The gold left was somewhat difficult to extract and the amounts taken far exceeded the needs of the miner civilization for their home planet. They sought to both store and sell the

72

remainder. What has been left on Earth, what mankind has found and extracted, is of little additional marginal value to the effort and estimated eventual worth."

The word "worth" suggests interplanetary trade. I can't imagine one part of the population of a planet, such as what we'd consider a sovereign nation like China, Russia, or the USA, would undertake interplanetary travel and mineral extraction without the knowledge or participation of all such people of the planet.

"That is correct," says The Committee, "the emergence of space transport across the galaxy almost never develops in a civilization where interplanetary trade is not imminent or already occurring. This is because the planet being seeded with the technology to develop interstellar transport will not misuse it, offers materials of its own and possible benefit from materials its neighbors might offer in return."

I am keen to know how the gold would be used and would those effects occur on Earth?

Say our friends on The Committee, "Yes, the gold dust would have a similar beneficial effect to Earth weather, as humans would perceive beneficial. Predictable weather, precipitation, storm pattern location and frequency offer benefits you understand well. The gold dust is milled to a particle weight that allows it to stay aloft without immediately falling or rising. It is first spread in an area of calm weather, and then as newer, unfilled calm areas of weather appear, more is spread. This evens out temperature fluctuation, reflecting incoming light and trapping planetary heat in fixed proportions. This evens out surface temperatures, because darkness, when nighttime heat radiation into space occurs, is also lessened. The result is smoothing of weather patterns, the intended effect."

I can only assume gold was chosen because of its resistance to oxidation and other possible atmospheric effects, to which The Committee replies, "Yes."

Now that we know what attracted ETs to create the first humanoids that evolved into humans to populate Earth as humans now do, we have to ask, what do the ETs want from here on forward, starting in the year of 2016?

Let's ask them.

"Greetings, this is Zebulon of Canopus here again, speaking in the collective voice of all of our civilization and on behalf of the many eagerly observing and looking forward to meeting some of you more closely.

"We say what we want simply is your companionship, in the ways we all shall agree each other's presence is beneficial. There are many routes this contact can take and we are prepared for all of them.

"We admire what has developed on Earth and now for the third time, and look forward to the continued development on Earth beyond the endings of the previously well-developed civilizations. The many routes of alternate stories Earth could have and has selected in alternate existence universes have not been followed or pursued in this Earth time sequence. Glad we are, for you shall soon know and see of other civilizations whose chosen courses have not served well their perpetuity and growth.

"It will be easy, simplistic, superficial, and incorrect to look upon us and believe that technology creates superiority, be it moral, scientific, and of any other form.

"The galaxy you have named for yourselves the Milky Way, it is ours also, it contains many, many civilizations whose physical development falls far newer along relative development than of Earth; you would not look upon any of them as inferior. You would be fascinated to discover and know of them, and as it will not distort or harm human life courses, we might well show and even take some of you to observe these places, much as we have come to observe yours.

"We understand some humans might fear us, an issue we cannot control. We frankly do not care about this, for we have not caused it. This is a human emotion we enjoy observing, where the human reactor can be seen by many a human observer to give away some responsibility, or credit or blame—at least, some involvement by examination of the newcomer's mere presence—for the reaction from which the strange newcomer has become known.

"We long ago discarded this approach to interpersonal reactions, and human ability to place responsibility for owned reactions upon mere existence and differences observed, this fascinates us.

"We have no joy, sorrow, regret, fear, or desire for any reaction to our presence, we are not emotionally attached to the reaction observers create in themselves. We are keenly interested in observation of the behavior and are grateful to mankind for allowing us the upcoming opportunity, as limited as it will be.

"We are not coming to colonize, occupy, control, dominate, mine, or affect Earth in any way. Were these our objectives, they would have already happened. The agreement we have all made to remain apart from and uninvolved in your development is made from a view toward selfish consistency; we wish to remain ourselves uncolonized, uninvaded, unoccupied, and undominated. We must give what we want, and do.

"Names for us we shall be given, and the existing and even new names for other ET friends of ours and yours, you might maintain and grant, the some of you. We use not names as mankind prefers, yet we gladly accept and even enjoy them, as you have allowed me to use the one Zebulon. We also like the name you have given our sun, Canopus.

"We want humanity to brave, surmount, and gain from the upcoming changes to Earth and the galaxy, forces of which now wash over Earth in greater and better waves than have in many, many centuries."

I have several questions for Zebulon and I ask.

I address our guest directly: Zebulon, a reader mentioned the death of a month's young human baby from malnutrition caused by war and famine, its mother unable to breast-feed in those conditions. The reader expressed curiosity at ET reaction to observance of such human suffering; I asked my guides, whose answer was that emotionality was not attached to human death and despair by visitor observers such as yourself and others from your colleague delegations. Can you explain what you see and feel when observing human tragedies, especially the self-generated or self-inflicted ones?

"Correct were your guides to say we are not emotionally attached, thus not sad, moved, perturbed, or otherwise negatively affected. This is not to suggest we have no care or empathy, for we do. We hold our presence and observation of Earth as a valuable prize and privilege; we cannot allow ourselves the misstep of reaction turned to interference, for this violates the agreement all visitors to Earth make. No approach or observation of Earth is permitted, if we might interfere; this is not a prohibition with sanctions, enforcement of infractions, or penalties, the way such rules are nearly universally applied on Earth. We may freely interfere and intervene, yet if we did, we would achieve two immediate and nearly permanent things; we would broadcast to any intruder upon our sanctity that all such interlopers are welcome to the opportunity to earn that status, at our expense, and worse, we would be seen as false, unreliable, and untrustworthy by all civilizations with whom we have, do, and might ever cross paths.

"This cost is so high, no willful violation is worth it.

"We understand many humans yearn for the appearance of someone to halt abuse and harm humans do to one another, the destruction of human well-being any one of you feels incapable of halting on your own. The sensation of being forced to stand helplessly by a problem, with no way to mitigate, solve, or prevent it, looms large in the good hearts of the many, the majority of you.

"To this we say, you have created your mess. Clean it up."

- 11 -
When Will They Come?

This is the biggest question many people have regarding the topic of this book. It's extremely important because how could anybody sell tickets without a date? Just imagine the torches and pitchfork crowd at the box office if an indefinite postponement were announced.

Apologies for disappointments, but the calendar date has not been scheduled and when it is, nobody on Earth is going to know until there is wildfire widespread knowledge.

Here I again ask The Committee for information about alien extraterrestrial arrival, and another extraterrestrial comes to the microphone. AE = alien extraterrestrial, C = The Committee.

Q: *OK, let's go to the ETs and ask them to inform us about when they will come.*
C: They have, already.

Q: *This leads to the first question! In what way will alien ETs reveal their presence in an unmistakable way humans cannot rationally deny; in other words, providing evidence to human senses that cannot be refuted. Can you ask a nearby alien ET visitor to please come address this?*
C: Indeed, allow us a few moments of your time on Earth to arrange this.

[A few minutes go by in Earth time, which I pass looking at a car magazine and vehicle which won't ever grace my driveway or backside, nice as it seems.]

AE: Thank you we do, how can we help?

Q: *The questioner is the respondent, tables turned.*
AE: In conversation, who is the interviewer or interviewee? Neither. Ask what you like.

Q: *We humans require labels and attach them, even of our own making if we don't get one we can comprehend. Who are you all, where are you, from where do you come?*

AE: Curiously we notice this, because we do the same. Classification and organization require it. We are from a set of planets in your and our quadrant of the galaxy. We are located closer to the center and our observance of Earth forms part of our exploration away from the center. We have done a large amount of exploration of the central core and now reach out towards the edge, beginning with our and your quadrant. We are orbiting Earth by hovering, in what you would call a synchronous orbit but we are not using your Earth's gravity to achieve this, although we could.

We are above what you call your southern Indian Ocean. We have no name you would understand.

Q: How many of you as individuals are aboard your ship or vessel?
AE: We are, as you would say, three dozen in number. We are not representative of our people but in the physical, just as human space travelers are not representative of many Earth inhabitants, not even closely.

Q: Do you specifically have plans to contact Earth and reveal yourselves to us?
AE: Most certainly not. We would happily do so but there are already plans in place for your closer neighbors to do this, who will. We would add nothing to the process but our own enjoyment, and likely cause confusion and difficulties. We ask you to consider a wedding ceremony or a funeral. If you are not invited, what do you add to the proceedings? Unlike ourselves, as humans you may attend if you remain quiet, display the appropriate appearance expected of all in attendance and participation and cause no disturbance. We would do this, simply by the reaction of our peers, our colleagues your fellow space traveler visitors.

Unlike such human social ceremonies or events, we can observe and extract as much information as we believe useful, without revelation of our physical selves.

Q: What humans wish to know is: WHEN are we going to see such galaxy visitors walk on our planet's surface and communicate with us?
AE: In a way the large majority will accept and believe; this has already happened and has many, many times over the course of human existence on Earth. In fact it has happened many times before humans were created and allowed to propagate.

Q: Allowed to propagate? As if we were going to be stopped?
AE: No, but this was possible. By leaving humans alone, this process

developed. There was no pattern of leaving Earth alone; it would barely resemble itself if plant then animal life had not been seeded on Earth by visitors such as ourselves.

Q: *Such as "ourselves?" Did your civilization have a hand in the placement of animal or plant life on Earth?*

AE: No, however many did. Mostly from your star cluster, however as you know from the other information this book supplies, the humans you are were created by a civilization far from your star cluster, which has not returned but to observe.

Q: *I do not need to mention how fearful and also misinformed to the point of tragic misguidance many of us are with the idea alien extraterrestrials would come to Earth.*

AE: But you have here made this mention.

Q: *Why don't I personally feel any worry or concern, or even much interest?*

AE: Into what many of your peers call your higher self we look, this is the aspect of your being you cannot well recognize when you are awake. You personally know this exists yet accept it is not a higher part of what has a lesser counterpart—you are not less than yourself in any way or form—and it is where your life plan or schedule, your budget of experience, resides. It holds forth this role for you personally, to establish the contact we now make together, and to help distribute our thoughts across humanity. When we say "our" we are most certainly not limiting this definition to our civilization, but rather we include all sovereign civilizations with plans to visit Earth and the few among them, to expose their presence on a large scale.

Q: *Are we going to see several different civilizations simultaneously?*

AE: No, there is a schedule and plan for each, to present themselves in order. Each will introduce the subsequent one, the greatest challenge will be the first.

Q: *How fast will this occur?*

AE: The pace of the roll out, as humans like to say, will depend almost entirely on humans. Your collective reaction. This cannot be controlled, and there is no desire to do so. Much human effort is made to predict economic activity and the ability to prosper in material, physical ways. Do economic forecasts turn out as well or as accurately as they suggest? The greater the audience, the less likely. The bigger the audience means the greater the collective belief. There will always be a segment or sector among the believers who will alter their behavior to either avoid what they deem loss, or secure greater proportional gain for themselves. These efforts alter the course of activity and change the outcome. The forecast is then deemed inaccurate when results are examined.

The challenge with forecasts involving human behavior is the assumption of reaction and the inability to establish a tipping or turning point created by collective changes to behavior. Much as chemistry successfully determines change points in titration, this cannot be done easily or at all, with human free will.

Thus human reaction to the widespread information that visitors such as ourselves indeed exist and can fly through your atmosphere, land upon your planet's surface and communicate with humans, will determine to the second group when and how they shall do the same.

How will you react to your aunt telling you at your age of twenty she is really your biological mother? How will your aunt, who you have always believed to be your mother, then present herself as no longer your mother? Will this information delivered by both women simultaneously become too much to manage or will you be indifferent to it? This is your choice. Will you reject them both as being dishonest to you during your entire life? Will you more easily accept this news first from your aunt you now know to be your biological mother, with nobody else present or aware? If you choose to accept it, will that make things easier for your aunt now known to be your mother, to come forward and speak with you in the newly revealed role? How fast or slow should this be done?

Your alien extraterrestrial cousins are very aware of this, and will not appear in a way likely to set off fears of an invasion. Panic will overwhelm many of you, if critical mass is reached. No purpose is served by this.

_Q:_   _Since the pace is determined by our reactions, when then will the first revelation take place?_

AE: It already has, the difference will be frequency and nature of them. Humans have taken keen notice of crop circles, designs and drawings but trip all over one another with absurd explanations which do not measure up to basic common sense, much less scientific examination. The default tendency as alien extraterrestrials are involved, is to reject and label any associated human as mentally unfit to some degree.

We take the current president of the nation the USA as an example for comparison. How many observers reject him in just this way and moreover, how many of such detractors rush to label, demean, criticize and worse, in very small numbers, even physically attack anyone not in agreement with their ideas? Yet the president is the president, chosen under an irrefutable system used dozens of times.

With great interest we observed the choosing of a leader for public policy and its execution, who had no prior, direct experience in the process. This was the appeal to supporters, who have by selecting such person for leadership, expressed dissatisfaction with the choices made over several previous elective cycles. The actions and reactions are most informative to watch. We suggest observance of athletic competitions, what are called sports, as similar. For us above all, the observance of human behavior resembles sporting competition.

We return to your question, these comparisons now drawn. The first revelation carried out in such way to seem like a first contact, which it will absolutely not be, will occur at some point human reaction to geophysical events reaches a critical phase.

We refer specifically to storms, earthquakes, volcanic eruptions, and changes to Earth's magnetic grid.

These events will come in clumps, groups, and series. Reactions to them will be as you can surmise, however the upswing of a new round of events after a calm period seen as the end of a round of bad events will spark fear and panic. Even humans aware of these changes, such you who now read these words, will be affected if by nothing more than watching the reactions, often of desperation, from others unaware of the process.

Alien ET contact will come at what is deemed the crucial thus ideal moment, shortly after a renewed series of events is feared. This will be done to provide explanations and reassurance, and even as some will desperately ask the first alien ET contactor to stop or control the geophysical events, these first contactors will explain how they are no more able to halt what happens than you humans are.

We shall remain in orbit and observe.

- 12 -
The Future of ETs with Earth

No pictures, photographs, diagrams, technical schematic drawings, or eyewitness accounts have been provided. It's the final chapter; is any "evidence" coming along in these last pages of the book? It looks like all we're getting we already have; no hidden files await in the appendix.

Saddled with what you've read, it is logical to ask, so what? Is this book just supposed to be filed away on the shelf like good entertainment, nothing more than a captivating mystery novel, or simply the next edition of a popular fantasy series, such as *Hairy Putter and The Ocean of Doubt*?

When the existence of extraterrestrial presence on Earth becomes unmistakable, your learning curve will be much flatter. Maybe even a downslope, which leads to the title of this chapter.

Given the technology extraterrestrials have and will demonstrate, such as ability to reach Earth from places we can't even determine exist, what will happen if we ask for cancer to be cured?

Yes, the medical technology to stop cancer (*the human body will effect reversal once the disease is halted, says The Committee*) exists with many extraterrestrials. They could "reverse" most war, nearly all weaponry, and do many other things. How wonderful to hand over the responsibility of arranging human society to someone other than humans. The solution to disease is cure; cancer isn't the only candidate condition. What about diabetes, cerebral palsy, multiple sclerosis, leprosy, heart disease, leukemia, Alzheimer's ... the list is not short. Why stop at cancer? In fact, how about we ask the extraterrestrials to arrange for fuel-free, zero-emissions energy production, and ... and ...

See where this goes and why we'll never get such "input"?

What is the future of ETs and Earth's human societies? What's the point of knowing about them?

My old and now your good friends on The Committee explain:

"To Earth you have come to live and to set aside for a time who you truly are. For this effective and intentional trip you have also temporarily put away things you already know and understand. Doubts and disbelief are your information storage cabinets.

"To Earth you have come to forget, then remember. Confusion and doubt are symptoms of the process, and if these things were not felt, you would not be where and who you are. Easy it is to flee from confusion and to seek certainty, even if attempts to depart are not swift and certainty is not reached. As any of you can remember, when leaving confusion behind, knowledge and experience come.

"Confronting confusion, with insistence to know its cause, pays great rewards when cleared up, as you are given to say. We offer that nothing has been cleared, it has been made transparent. When gaining knowledge, you are remembering. You already know what you believe you do not know, then learn. If becoming a doctor seems difficult or impossible, this feeling is produced by your knowledge of medical treatment and ability to perform it, well concealed within your soul.

"If confusion and doubt are left aside, and certainty pursued, how long will this condition remain before seeing new doubts, challenges, and confusions appear? As you all know, new things appear steadily and constantly in everyone's life. There will always be confusing moments, combinations of great knowledge and ability not seen previously.

"Mankind on Earth lives at a unique time, when great changes flow through the universe and galaxy. Such effects have not washed over your planet for hundreds of centuries along the Earth timeline. This time marks a change human life has not yet experienced: integration.

"Earth will discover its place among its neighbors and in the galaxy. More will be understood about your galaxy's place among its many companions. These companions have always watched over you, examined you, and monitored your many moves.

"The population of Earth approaches its zenith and will decline in the coming decades. Many of you reading this will see the decline occur. The excitement to live on Earth and gain the experience of the changes from where you are, are valued in ways that cannot be expressed in human language and perception.

"Humanity has learned to play with matches without understanding the fires which can result. We refer to nuclear energy, a key part of technology your extraterrestrial cousins have developed. This is one area of interference coordinated between your extraterrestrial cousins, their own soul guides, and the guardians and all of the guides each of you are blessed to ask then have join you, along your human journey.

"The use of nuclear energy for weapons has already caused effects and disrup[t] far beyond Earth and into realms humans do not perceive. These effects ar[e] positive and will not be permitted to repeat or worsen.

"Preferable would it have been to demonstrate the benefits of the unlocking of this energy before its application to kill, yet no power over mankind can prevent development. This is not allowed. Destruction of Earth's environment, making it inhabitable, is within the power humans allow yourselves, before you choose to incarnate and journey across Earth's surface.

"Slowly and steadily shall come the contacts from the several civilizations of which you are already aligned, with whom Earth already shares a relationship it does not recognize. Not yet.

"The history of humanoid life on Earth will be explained as has been done briefly in this short book, and then humanity will understand its place. The reasons no contact has been initiated, until now, will be understood.

"Not everything your extraterrestrial cousins have done fits the human interpretation of positive; there have been cases of animals mutilated for examination and research, the remains left behind, then found. No harm to humanity has been intended and none intentionally done.

"The sensation of control and the discomfort of its perceived absence will undergo a great change among humans. It is easy to feel fear, concern, and discomfort with things unfamiliar, especially that which you have never seen or known. You have both taught yourselves and learned well, in your Earth environment, and skeptical have grown the many of you within it. Habit extends this skepticism and it will be applied to extraterrestrial presence, and fear will have opportunity to grow from it.

"Fear undermines your well-being, as all of you already know. Short bursts of it, in risky situations, protect you. Ongoing fear does not, and we say, ongoing fear is not possible without desire. To suffer with it over long periods requires the affirmative participation of the frightened, although human behavior discounts and even denies this. The many of you can accurately point to examples of such fear and suggest our description places blame on the victim. To this we say, yes. Over time, a victim indeed earns the fear disliked.

"Fear is one of the greatest motivators toward understanding and resolution, for growth and a strengthening of the soul. For this you experience it and design it into your human personality, mentality, and lives. Just as hunger motivates the search for food, fear motivates the search for relief, often most quickly obtained with understanding.

"We speak of this because we know it will be an immediate and common emotion, and we see it as opportunity knocking upon the personal front door of any and all humans who experience this emotion upon knowing of extraterrestrial cousins.

"Upon first discovery of irrefutable extraterrestrial evidence, this will be known through eyewitness photographs, such encounters planned to make ET presence known. There will be great doubt, skepticism, and condemnation of the photographs and accounts of the meetings. This is the objective, to see encounters occur with absence of fear.

"It is expected, even planned, that humans will be doubtful and dismissive of stories told by the few humans encountered by extraterrestrials in an open way. These encounters, and their descriptions and photographs, will continue to happen in such a way that dismissal of them as hoaxes, frauds, and faked encounters will become very difficult.

"Casual, personal human photography has become almost entirely digital, which more easily allows deception, although this is difficult. When these digitized images are offered, they will be declared elaborate hoaxes. As accounts of extraterrestrial presence spread, indeed imitators will create hoaxes, in the attempt to gain from the notoriety occurring.

"There will be chemical photographs made, the previously common technology no longer popular and more difficult to falsely create. As the reports of encounters increase, it will become obvious the vast majority of humans involved lack ability to concoct false information and evidence.

"As this occurs, there will be attempts to lure extraterrestrials, who need no incentive. There will be given responses to the invitations to make contact, by the extraterrestrials. As these responses are given, away from yet with specific knowledge of the invitation, it will become undeniable to examination that something indeed is creating the replies to human calls for more contact.

"From this point forward, more and regular contact will occur. Mankind will select the course of this development; your extraterrestrial visitors are not here to assist, instruct, control, manipulate, influence, or create anything humanity would not otherwise do for, by, and to itself.

"They have come simply and precisely to welcome Earth's developing societies to the conference.

"Prepare for these discussions, both your questions and your open mind for answers you cannot now know to expect. What you will learn of faraway worlds and histories of developments upon and between planets cannot be suggested, so interesting and detailed will be the information.

"Knowledge of materials, elements, wars, animal and plant life and hybrids of the two humans have speculated exist will be seen to indeed thrive on many worlds in your galaxy. The histories of worlds far less developed than Earth will be explained, and the parallels to Earth development compared. Likewise there will be an accounting of the extraterrestrials and their own historical developments as they reached similar stages of social and scientific development Earth now enjoys.

"More telling will be the many different courses of development each of your close cousin and neighbor civilizations have followed, from similar points along their paths of growth. Earth society will understand its choices in a way not able to be understood from the illusion of fixed-time process as it applies to all of you.

"Forward shall you progress, confident in the ways you can select and proceed, equipped with knowledge only experience develops. Much as mankind created the notion of a nation-state and began sharing information with others seen as previously disengaged, shall Earth become the nation-state of just one civilization, now seen to be futile or impossible. Indeed, among you are the many who dislike, others who abhor, the concept of national sovereignties wiped away while others embrace it with a passion rarely seen outside personal love.

"This view is likely among the first to come under scrutiny once knowledge of development has been shared with mankind, as to what opportunities and obstacles were encountered on other worlds and among civilizations of other solar systems. Yours contains today only yourselves, in your dimensionality; no longer are there humanoids on Mars and never have there been humanoid civilizations on the remaining planets, even the destroyed ones which remain as asteroids.

"The human desire for integration of sovereign nations does not emphasize responsibility or change, the modification of one's own preferences as the benefits of the integration are pursued. This is what reigns now on Earth; the European Union is an excellent example and its imminent disintegration will result from an approach which prefers the benefits without an equally close examination of the factors which create the benefits preferred, and the responsibilities attaching to those factors.

"Objections to dissolved national sovereignties are correct to resist; however, the true reason such objections hold value is as we have described in the previous paragraph.

"Extraterrestrials will explain what obstacles and solutions have been attempted and which succeeded or failed, and the process of extracting great benefit from failure. It teaches far more than success and when this aspect of life is given equal standing in human Earth behavior, so will humanity have advanced a great leap into the next phase of its development.

"A great greeting we both wish and send to all of you, who have read our words here, who have absorbed through them our thought energy, for words we do not use. We observe them transcribed, that which we say with our minds, and in parting, for now, we also wish to say, we wish you a great and bountiful trip."

Postface

Although it might seem otherwise, the author is not that interested in ET visitors. Some people, and I will suggest there are many, want to see them immediately and if possible, by yesterday. The idea contact with ETs is possible will set off a gold rush of spectators like free cash handed out at city hall. No, that would be a stampede now that I think about it; it won't be that intense. Aside from a few tramplings, however, it will probably not be much different.

I do not wish to have much contact with ETs although I confess great interest in their histories and the why and how of the certain aspects they considered negative, which were improved or overcome. The application of their concepts and solutions to humankind interests me a good deal. That's the study of history, of course, which always holds forth promise for brighter futures.

Knowing how ET-determined habits, behaviors, customs, and traditions were not good then eliminated represents, for me, hope we can always find a better way forward, as human history shows we have successfully done many times, if not always, throughout.

I do not care much for ET spaceships or to see their home planets. I am not that interested in their uses of technology or joy rides at Warp 8. I am, however, keenly interested in the ways the human race can apply new concepts on Earth, for things such as disease, pollution, peace, poverty, and so forth. I realize I am in the minority and that a larger majority, if willing to invest beliefs, might enjoy a book like this.

You now have enough knowledge for an informed reaction to the news of extraterrestrial visitors. It will be offered; it's only a matter of time.

Appendix

This book was read by a few hundred people before publishing, as chapters and portions of them were posted on the author's website. This appendix contains select anonymous questions and comments to chapters 3 through 12. Because the questions did not originate with the author, spirit beings, or alien extraterrestrials, the author believes they are best presented as an addendum rather than accompany each chapter. The titles of each chapter have been included.

In some cases, the questioner's name is withheld to protect identity; however, mostly first names and some initials were used when the comments and questions were posted, anonymity thus already in effect. The dates and clock times, displayed in military or British format (date/month/year), are included to establish the timeline during which these reader and author exchanges took place.

You might find this additional information as interesting as the chapters themselves, as have many readers. Alien ETs are a topic which generates enthusiastic interest, the display of which informs anyone even mildly curious, and for having read this far, likely includes you.

Chapter 3 - Let's Talk With One

Yang 22 March 2016 06:21:33

Q: *I would love to interpret ETs for others, in a way we are doing now.*
AE: You can do so all you like, where others will listen. Will they?

Q: *What I mean is in a live, in-person Q&A session.*
AE: Assemble your audience, we will answer any question or explain why we cannot or do not explain.
Q: *I don't know how to do it and don't feel much urge to do so.*
AE: Then allow others to make the arrangement and contact you.

Q: *OK, it would be a lot of fun and faster than typing.*
AE: Yes.

Q: *Yes, do a live interview!*
       What did you mean by Q3—I don't feel much urge to do so?
       Can you record in any way? Allowed? If not—why?

I see other mediums can get pictures and see how the person they channel look like, but this is different to you? AE can't send you a picture to describe how they look like?

Patrick 22 March 2016 11:02:16

1. To make a video recording of a session, I have neither the location or equipment, nor means to obtain even the use of them. As some of you know, I did two YouTube videos of a session but they seemed (to me) to be too slow and nothing more than simply the "reading out loud" of what would end up written down anyway. My voice doesn't add any meaning to the message, as I see it.
2. I don't feel the urge to set up a physical meeting, where guests would be invited to ask questions I would answer. The mechanics and logistics of making such arrangements I feel little impulse to organize and set up. Somebody else would have to do it. I would not do a good job. (I know from old experience, others are better at this function.) That also doesn't address the publicity and advertising, essential component(s) of the process.

Yang 25 March 2016 01:52:08

Ah, a "channeling" meeting. I initially thought you/they meant a face-to-face meeting as in, "What I mean is in a live, in-person Q&A session." I agree that a channeling Q&A would not be nearly the same. My mistake, I misunderstood.

Chapter 4 - More Examples

BK 20 March 2016 16:02:04

So, the question is sort of, "why don't aliens join the earthling rebel alliance instead of the awful Empire when the rebel alliance is clearly on the side of right?" The answer provided is good. It's not another civilization's place to take sides.

BK 20 March 2016 16:27:34

A question tacked on a comment. This says, "You have been placed in the center of a great wilderness with all features of Earth as you know them; forests, valleys, mountains, rivers, plains and otherwise.

You travel outward and eventually reach the edge of the wilderness, which is finite."

And also recently, "many of you have incarnated as ETs."

Are all/many/most/no humans tied to a race destiny/evolutionary path as a group? Or are the bodies spirit selects completely up to choice/arbitrary?

Are all/many/most/no "ETs" tied to a race destiny/evolutionary path as a group on their home planet?

Or do we all just get around according to preference?

Patrick 22 March 2016 11:11:35

Questions repeated and numbered:

1.   Are all/many/most/no humans tied to a race destiny/evolutionary path as a group?
1a.   Or are the bodies spirit selects completely up to choice/arbitrary?
2.   Are all/many/most/no "ETs" tied to a race destiny/evolutionary path as a group on their home planet?
3.   Or do we all just get around according to preference?

Says The Committee:

1.   Many; however, there is no race destiny but for the human perception of racial groups, whose limits, when defined by humans, always either include or exclude many millions of you as the group's definitions are sharpened or relaxed.
1a.   Not arbitrary, each soul considers its body individually but often with consideration of the group into which the life plan is arranged.
2.   There are too many distinct ET civilizations to answer this correctly and succinctly.
3.   Yes, however there are many influences considered, which together can make it seem as if there is a group consideration which overrides the individual choice. The eventual choice any person makes is always a combination. The proportions vary greatly from one soul to another.

BK 23 March 2016 16:02:44

Thank you for the translation of my questions into logical form and for the replies!

Suds 20 March 2016 16:59:22

Again, great work, Patrick. Looking forward to getting the whole book. One thought currently intrigues me—how can you make jokes when your counterpart has telepathic knowledge about the very twist that creates the fun of it? Is this finally a treat that is unique to us humans?

Suds 21 March 2016 02:35:11

So taking this thought a little bit further and generalizing a bit: creativity— often it is a result of mental privacy, as one might call it. Of course creativity often depends on inspiration, discussion and interaction, with other individuals. But then there is the phase when you might seek solitude with your thoughts, when you want to be undisturbed, chewing on a problem that you want to solve, when you are under the shower preparing yourself for the enlightening idea … For some people (and I count me in) creativity requires oscillation between secluded privacy and being out in the open with others.

Maybe a provocative question having in mind an intelligent being that does communicate by telepathy—can these beings experience mental solitude? Do they experience creativeness the way we do? How do they hide the funny surprise until the point when you need it when cracking a joke? Is this also a reason why it is so special to be a human?

Patrick 22 March 2016 11:18:00

Says The Committee: "Telepathic ability is not license or permission to enter another person's thoughts at the sole will of the listener. To eavesdrop is not generally possible; the characteristics of human speech and sound waves do not have such check or control, as does operate with the energetic waves of thoughts and communication."

Patrick 22 March 2016 11:14:41

Says The Committee: "Thoughts are read the way speech is heard. The telepathic ability to communicate does not allow the telepathic listener to reverse sequence, in order to know the thoughts of the counterpart in communication, before those thoughts are formulated."

Steve 20 March 2016 19:05:35

Gosh, I'm thinkin, let's just get this first contact (Take 2) over and done with already, half time break next Super Bowl just spring up from understage (ala Michael Jackson) and say "Surprise, we're back!!"

Susie S 21 March 2016 21:14:47

I feel Michael Jackson was a starperson meaning he was 1/3 Starperson ,1/3 Angel qualities and 1/3 Wise one, and possibly from Venus :-) Am I right Committee? ;-) Says The Committee: "Pure ET's or Starpeople have never incarnated to Earth but prefer to visit on scout ships."

Steve 22 March 2016 05:08:52

Me thinks he was the biggest star this planet will ever see in a flesh suit.

Susie S 22 March 2016 15:12:31

Yes, MJ incarnated being very close and connected to Source energy. He came to light up the world :-)

Patrick 22 March 2016 11:20:09

The Committee: "Within a human view or a soul's hierarchy, your view holds value. Move above and away from the human categorization of Heaven and the galaxy's organization, and the view is altered."

Name Withheld 21 March 2016 23:23:22

I have several questions:

1.   Are the ETs from the same dimension as ours (3D) and from different galaxies/star systems? Or are there ETs from different dimensions as well?
2.   What does a different dimension look like? Is "heaven" or the "spiritual world" just a different dimension?
3.   How many dimensions are there?
4.   If there are other dimensions, do these dimensions have different universes and galaxies? Or is there only one universe and different dimensions in it?
5.   The "Heaven" … where is this situated? Is there a different spirit world for different planets? Or is there a common spirit world irrespective of the planets and aliens?
6.   Can a 5-dimensional being visit a 3-dimensional world and survive?
7.   Are some aliens that we see actually robots? Is it possible for soul to enter a mechanical/electrical/artificial body created by intelligent being?
8.   I read somewhere that an old civilization from the time of Atlantis went to live underground. Is that true? If so, how advanced is this civilization? Do they have contacts with aliens as well? Do they have "UFOs?"
9.   Are there underground bases of aliens on the earth? Where?
10.   How different are silicon-based organisms from carbon-based ones? Silicon-based compounds are not as stable and varied as carbon-based ones. Do we have any silicon-based organism on Earth? How different is a silicon-based one from our world? What do they breathe?

Patrick 22 March 2016 11:33:03

1.   No, the visitors to Earth are from higher vibrational ranges within OUR dimensionality and also transpose in to higher (faster) vibrations or dimensions we cannot perceive. Depends on which civilization.
2.   Heaven is the next two "levels up" from where we are. It would require an encyclopedia to describe what it looks like, accurately.
3.   Approximately ten, depending on how dimensions are defined. Upon entering the higher levels, the number of them decreases. From the first three and four, it is ten. From the 9th or 10th, there are less.
4.   No and there are different universes, also. The dimensions and the universe do not correlate. It's like asking if there are different continents and family trees in societies upon each.
5.   Heaven surrounds us, and we are in it all the time. No, the spiritual worlds for different planets is the same, just as the planets also occupy the same galaxy.
6.   Yes. A 5th dimension being is our soul. The physical limits of a 3rd dimension environment do not apply or affect it.
7.   No, ETs have not brought or demonstrated androids, although they have them. These are, to ET civilizations the ones which visit us, just tools and machines. No, a soul cannot "live" inside a mechanical device.
8.   No.
9.   No.
10.   Very different from the silicon compounds known on Earth. The ones to be discovered will be a chemistry revelation. No, we do not have silicon-based life on Earth.

Yang 22 March 2016 06:14:11

They mentioned that they approved your request to make an interview face-to-face (if I understood it correctly?). Which would be awesome. Now, are you allowed to tape it, record it, photo it? If not—why?

Patrick 22 March 2016 11:21:24

"They" = The Committee or ETs?

Yang 31 March 2016 09:12:57

The ET's. However, I already got the answer to this earlier. I thought they meant face to face as in person to person LIVE with an audience. Maybe naive, but one can dream :)

Steve 26 March 2016 18:57:26

I must say before your books turn you into a famous man Patrick, I have enjoyed these readings immensely!

Chapter 5 - Their Homes

Denis 15 March 2016 19:21:22

Zebulon of Canopus—The Extraterrestrial adventure, intrigue, wonder

The Alien Handbook—A Guide to Extraterrestrials a manual of operation, of understanding, of knowledge

Steve 15 March 2016 19:22:39

Maybe talk to Doug Adams estate, and do a co deal on Hitchhikers Guide To The Inhabitants Of the Galaxy!!, nah just kidding

Yang 15 March 2016 21:34:10

Telepathic communication can't dissolve spoken language entirely, can it? For example, a book—how is it constructed without a language of speak? And if books exist, then what language is used? Is English prevalent in other planets than Earth? Is there a broadly used written language in the Universe?

Patrick 16 March 2016 18:26:11

Yes, telepathy disposes of the need for speech and listening.

Written words are simply graphs of speech, and came about on Earth long after speech was developed. The written word influences speech once literacy is achieved; however, none of us learns to speak our native tongues through writing.

Telepathic beings provide the equivalent of what we would call books in the form of diagrams, pictures, and illustrations with telepathic communication built into the images. As a telepathic "book" is read, its messages are conveyed much as we humans read and comprehend word clusters and thoughts they represent. I just did that, to provide this message. My transliteration of the information involves putting into human words the information I am given.

Yang 16 March 2016 20:29:38

Telepathy is a world as fascinating as it is unknown to me, yet makes me thrilled about its existence and the depth of knowledge it carries. I reckon that albeit the ability to communicate telepathically is within us all, only a few are gifted to unlock its secrets. Like you Patrick. Thanks for sharing with us.

Mike 16 March 2016 11:29:19

Although I'm sure they are aware. How do most alien races feel about Western Governments attempts to stage a fake alien invasion. As I'm sure it will have lots of implications for the genuine visitors out there.

Project Bluebeam

http://www.disclose.tv/news/Project_Bluebeam_US_Government_Planning_a_False_Flag_With_UFOs/91136

Patrick 16 March 2016 18:27:32

The Committee says this is speculation; there are no plans to stage false ET appearances for effect, by established governments.

Denis 16 March 2016 12:10:51

Canopus—A Distant World
Canopus—Extraterrestrial Civilisation
Zebulon—Talks of Life on Canopus
Zebulon—Conversation with a Canopian or an Extraterrestrial Life on Canopus: Extraterrestrials

Mike 16 March 2016 16:10:28

I also wanted to ask, are there any alien races that call any of the planets in our Solar System home?

So they would either exist in another dimension or the media keeps it hidden from us?

Patrick 16 March 2016 18:19:31

No and yes, many things are in different dimensions, but no, there is no media cover-up.

Chapter 6 - Physical Appearance

Steve 18 March 2016 17:39:55

Thanks Pat,

Can I ask do they 1) utilise showering, 2) produce pungent body odor like us?

Patrick 19 March 2016 10:27:09

I take the question to be about the ETs which have contacted Earth beings (humans) in recent times.

1.   Not much and it is done mostly for refreshment and relaxation as much as for removal of dead skin cells, perspiration, sebum, etc.

2.   No, not that we can detect. The body chemistry is much different. The bacteria that cause this in humans does not operate the same way with these visitors. If the ET visitors were to stay in the Earth environment for long enough and alter their diet also, this could happen.

Steve 19 March 2016 16:39:12

This is so interesting, can I ask in regards to Denis no 4) Why weren't they smart enough to suss out very early, that they were trying to approach the wrong bunch of humans, who would not be genuinely interested in helping humanity? It really doesn't do much to instill in me that they are so intelligent.

Patrick 19 March 2016 21:31:49

Chapters 3 and 4 discuss this.

Denis 18 March 2016 19:01:38

Overall in a century 5 races have visited,

1-   Does that explain the different designs of crop circles?
2-   Does each race use a different symbolism in their designs?
3-   How many human meetings were done in the past century?
4-   Have they produced anything positive for them in their meetings other than study of the body and mind?
5-   What chemical smell would be similar to their body odor?
        I notice Stonehenge in the header pic, a preview of the next chapter?

Patrick 19 March 2016 10:30:53

1.   Partially, but the crop circles have also been done by visitors not making contact with humans.
2.   Yes.
3.   Dozens and dozens.
4.   Positive for the ETs? Not much. The purpose is help humanity, provide a benefit to mankind, which has generally been resisted.
5.   The faint odor of burned silicon electronic components. Stonehenge is in coming chapters, yes.

Denis 19 March 2016 15:27:27

Thank you Patrick,
A very interesting handbook.

Susie 18 March 2016 19:02:41

Interesting :-) I call ET's … Starpeople or Star person.

Patrick 19 March 2016 10:32:19

Star Trek, Star Wars … star people! Logical.

Mike 19 March 2016 13:35:21

You mention that most alien visitors to our world are silicon based. Does this equate to us actually meeting androids rather than living, breathing beings like humans? As silicon is the major composite of our technological world. Just as AIs are different to humans.

We may make them in our image, give them human abilities. But they will never be human.

Patrick 19 March 2016 14:21:54

No. Silicon is the key element in the compounds that make up the physical and environmental chemistry of some ETs, in the same way carbon does this in the Earth environment and its living beings. Compounds such as carbohydrates (food), air (carbon dioxide), and also hydrocarbon compounds (fuel).

Many silicon compounds provide good control of electricity flow, hence the term semiconductor, electrical circuit components which contain silicon-based compounds.

There is some overlap, because the silicon-based nature of the ET body chemistry means at some point we are going to discover a very interesting feature of the nervous system network of the ET physiology. (The Committee told me this last part.)

Eva 19 March 2016 15:44:32

This information about ETs is so compelling. It really makes it so realistic, which it is of course. I wonder, and this may sound trite or superficial, but do they (ETs) have ideals of what we humans would describe as a beautiful face and/or body? From my human standpoint, I cannot say that they look beautiful, as they are being described. Do we look less than beautiful to them then?

Patrick 19 March 2016 21:34:29

Beauty is HIGHLY subjective, but overall, we are seen as beautiful to the ET visitors much more than a majority of us might regard ETs that way.

Mike 19 March 2016 21:13:29

Another question if I may then. I read an interview of someone who had been to a secure base where alien craft are kept (think it was Dulce). Anyway whilst travelling through the tunnels they happened upon a room that had what appeared to be part of an engine from a craft. The guy commented that it looked like a regular engine part, but when he went to touch it it moved like it was alive. He said it felt like it was aware and responded to his touch. Yet it was used to propel an ET craft.

Does this apply to all their technology, that somehow it connects with its pilots and is much more than just mere propulsion. Instead an extension of the ET pilot's being.

Patrick 19 March 2016 21:37:09

Says The Committee: "In some cases, with some spacecraft from some civilizations, YES."

As I read your description Mike, The Committee "played the video" for me, of this very thing happening.

Chapter 7 - Technologies

Name Withheld 25 March 2016 23:33:59

More questions as usual …

Q1: *Do ETs indulge themselves in songs and music like humans? For those who have lost the ability to speak, I guess singing is out of question.*

C: Of course they do and, no, it is not beyond ability. It is common to do. Singing is poetry set to rhythm, words matched to music. Speech is not is not common among your extraterrestrial friends, because of the efficiency of telepathic thoughts. These are easy to match to music. A A human habit of hearing words sung with vocal chord sounds does not mean thoughts intended to communicate messages are not aligned with musical rhythms. If fact, mankind would be surprised and almost shocked to understand the depth and diversity of ET songs, lyrics, and messages set to music.

Q2: *Do our thoughts emit some kind of energy which could be detected by the ETs? If there is some kind of energy, does it operate in a different dimensional/vibrational range which is why we can't detect it with our devices?*

C: Thoughts are energy, one and the same. Yes, thoughts are received well by ETs, and also by humans. You call it intuition, mind reading, channeling and often, just a hunch. Thought energy transcends all dimensions. It is not detected by human devices because none are required. Your brain and soul do it far more easily and efficiently. The human habit and custom of speech give the appearance otherwise.

Q3: *From how far can the ETs monitor the thoughts of an individual on earth? Do they have specialized devices to capture the thoughts or do they do it with their own brain?*

C: ETs in physical bodies can generally do it from up close to orbit about your planet, if they focus on a specific person or group. In the reverse, if a human directs thoughts to an extraterrestrial, the human thoughts sent will be received farther than this. The directness of communication is supported by belief it exists, that it functions and in deed and fact communicates. This greatly extends the range. To the outer edges of your solar system.

Q4: *Can ETs record, store and play back thoughts of humans?*

C: Yes, these are called memories. Do humans not also do this? We understand you mean a physical recording, which reproduces sound.

Thoughts are not sound and thus are far easier to remember, recall, and repeat.

Q5:   *Is it possible for ETs to visualize, smell or hear events occurring in Earth's past? For example, if they want to see exactly what happened in ancient Rome in a particular room of a palace at a particular point of time, can they "tune" into it?*

C: Yes. The recall often derives from the soul energetic persona involved in the events, if that and those souls wish to replay the scene for the inquirer. This operates for humans also; you call these vivid memories. You can ask a memory to be replayed for you. This is common among humans. Even more so with extraterrestrials, who rely upon the same source of information as do humans. The difference is, ETs do not doubt the source and content to nearly the extent humans assume doubt is prudent."

Q6:   *Some people say that pointed structures like the pyramids or the Washington monument serve as transmitters of earth events for ETs? Is this true?*

C: Yes, as are trees and many taller objects, even mountains. The human-built structures are either inadvertent transmitters or were designed and erected intentionally, from soul memory, purpose, and agreement, even if the motivators behind the projects are not consciously aware. The monument you mention, an obelisk, is a transmitter and marker much as are the pyramids of Egypt, Mexico, and many others on Earth. The Washington obelisk is capped with aluminum for this purpose. Texas has another, and also Argentina. Many more exist, for similar dual purposes.

Q7:   *Some UFO abductees have claimed that ETs have implanted devices in their brains. If true, what's the purpose of devices if thoughts could be monitored directly from the brain?*

C: No, there are no permanent cerebral devices. These would be found and made known, if there were. No such devices are required to monitor thought energy; the brain does not serve this function. It is a compiler and translator of thought to physical motion, be that the physical movement producing sound waves of speech, or converting sound waves to thought energy. Language processor is a good name for the brain. Human brains receive electrical signals created from sound and convert the signal to thought energy required for understanding. You do not hear with your brain, but rather the soul. The brain is the energy-to-body interface.

Q8:   *Have there ever been intergalactic wars between ET civilizations?*

C: Yes.

Q9:   *Is there a "galactic federation" sort of thing among ET civilizations like we see in "Star Trek"?*

C: Many, thousands in just your galaxy. They are arranged from local to larger areas, much as government entities, agencies, and branches are created and organized in human societies.

Q10:   *When huge distances could be travelled using "space compression" what happens to the time in respect of the traveller? Einstein's theory says that when we travel at near light speeds, time dilation happens. So if the ET vessel takes 2 hours to arrive at earth and 2 more hours to go back, what amount of time is elapsed at their planet? Will it be 4 hours or less or more? Similarly, is there any change in the mass of their spaceships?*

C: This answer requires us to ask, then answer, what is time? Earth life in a dense physical body participates in the dark and day cycles, and the measurement of the cycles creates the impression of time, as each appearance of sunlight is numbered. The cycle is divided in segments, sub-segments, and so forth. Stationary hovering above Earth, so that the sun is always at the same angle, erases time.

ETs also have a form of this measurement on each planet, which does not match the Earth rhythms. The amount of time that elapses depends on the planet of origin's pace of rotation. In some cases, it is two to one, in others one to two, yet there are many variations.

When humans approach then exceed three hundred thousand kilometers per second, time as Earth presence perceives it to exist, fades away. This does not mean human body functions are suspended, but rather the calendar of Earth and the devices called clocks which measure sub-segments cease to be relevant.

When a traveler returns to the environment of origin, such beings will encounter elapsed time according to their own pace of measurement, as would occur with an Earth dweller after travelling through outer space.

Mass is a relative measure of density, relevant to the gravity field into which it is inserted. ET ships which remain in orbit avoid the effects of changes to density; scout ships also, but they compensate for the differences they know shall be encountered. For the few ETs walking on Earth, the differences are adjusted where the change will otherwise cause them to be too light or heavy. The adjustments are achieved by use of gravity neutralization or adjustment devices. Just as gravity can be neutralized, it can also be increased or reduced. The way electricity can be varied in strength.

Yang 29 March 2016 01:07:14

I just want to add to the general public that "E.T" is such a wide concept that we literally are trying to collectively conceptualize billions of civilizations into one word. This is rather narrow minded—We could equally say "Animals on earth, how do they look?" and that would be an understatement in comparison.

We must understand that ET as a term basically means all life outside Earth in all dimensions, where we are the clear minority. Thus, whatever we have— THEY have. Whatever THEY have, we probably don't. We live in a limited world, with limited thinking with limited resources. A 2 year old can easily point out flaws in this world; war, sicknesses, greed, hate, jealousy and general ego-mentality—all choices we have made in one way or the other. And because in the other dimensions, humans can be 2 km tall, the concept of reality for us and reality to them is highly changeable, all physical and mental aspects are just off the charts. If YOU can imagine it—it exists.

NOTE: Mass and weight are two different things (in Earth-terms). Mass is the amount of atoms that makes for the object, while Weight only exists when there is a gravity pulling on that object, thus Mass is independent of gravity as defined on Earth. Also, they are both scalars—one dimensional units, alas, density is not, which is a two-dimensional unit. I just want to clarify that the text could be confusing if applied in earth scientific terms.

Patrick 29 March 2016 21:57:03

Well said, and The Committee adds a comment: "What does mass without gravity mean to humans?"

Yang 31 March 2016 09:17:29

2 apples are the same 2 apples anywhere in the physical Universe. This because MASS is the SAME. Move the same specific apples around in the Universe and WEIGHT will change. Thus, mass without gravity means that eating the mass comparable to 2 apples with zero weight can still make you full.

Patrick 31 March 2016 10:56:17

Says The Committee; "Mankind will be fascinated to discover the constancy of mass is variable across the galaxy. This is a great discovery all will enjoy."

Steve 29 March 2016 18:25:59

I wonder if ETs enjoy any human music or performers?

Patrick 29 March 2016 21:55:35

Says The Committee, "YES! They do and it is among the reasons Earth is visited. It is a strong attraction. Invisible attendance at human performances would fill stadiums unable to be imagined."

Steve 30 March 2016 07:01:47

Wow, that's cool, I'm thinking more so Kenny and Dolly, than Marilyn Manson.

Yang 28 March 2016 05:33:38

Equally mind-blowing and confusing—yet so fascinating. Good work and thank you Patrick!

Janis 28 March 2016 13:13:06

Q1:   *Do ET's access knowledge (science) as a collective resource as they need it or do they learn it like ourselves?*

C: Both, just as you do and have on Earth. As humans share information among nations, so do your extraterrestrial cousins among many civilizations.

Q2:   *Are the Et's on the ship more like our military personnel? Is there a commander?*

C: There is a well-defined organization which resembles a human military unit, yes. Yes, there is a commander. These visitors are not military minded, they are explorers, emissaries, and ambassadors. Earth is not the sole or even high-priority mission, in many cases. The defense capabilities are for protection of both humans and the visitors. Their abilities are used to disable and prevent human use of force, thus removing the need for protection beyond prevention and avoidance of harm to all sides.

   Close study of the visitors' teams would lead humans to understand them as anthropologist explorers and diplomats.

Q3:   *Are the elder ETs the ones that are responsible for the decisions to go to a certain planet? Are they elected or is it based on their longevity and experience?*

C: Yes, there are chosen leaders and representatives and often alliance involvement in the planning of Earth visits and observations. There are many considerations given to the selection of leaders of such civilizations, and Earth visits are rarely given much value in leadership selection. Chosen leadership will designate an envoy to the galactic alliances, one with authority to commit to study, including visits, to and of civilizations not aligned with a galactic conference. Such as Earth.

Q4: *Does the committee know the individuals who are actively reading and participating on this site.*

C: Yes, we know of all of you.

Q5: *Whenever I read the words of the committee I feel this emotional pull. Familiar but just out of my reach. Just a comment.*

C: You are not out of reach, your human training creates this. The emotional pull you feel is your true self poking through the wrapping. The human word is channeling, you are feeling the beginnings of telepathic communication natural to you.

kathi hast 28 March 2016 21:04:10

Thank you Patrick. I am so pleased that I lived to be so old and have begun learning more about our world.

Patrick 29 March 2016 23:04:55

None of us are old; time is an illusion. You're most welcome.

Chapter 8 - History of ETs on Earth

Steve 2 April 2016 01:42:01

The original 7 Level system of Reiki involves the drawing of several symbols, but there doesn't seem to be a definitive explanation of the origins of the symbols, and the energy of Reiki itself, I'm assuming this must be an "ET" thing?

Patrick 2 April 2016 12:08:41

Reiki is "also" an ET thing (it's "ours," too) which includes many beings from many civilizations across the galaxy and universe. Some of the things ETs could explain about it are indeed what you mention, Steve.

Steve 2 April 2016 20:23:03

Thanks Pat,

Reiki is hugely popular, dare I suggest another possible spin off book, The origins of Reiki explained by ET's by P De Haan, and if released in timely fashion, the beard grown could again be utilised

Name Withheld 2 April 2016 04:47:47

So there are messages in crop circle patterns. But so far nobody has been able to decipher them. What good do these messages serve if nobody is able to understand what they mean? Any clue on how to decipher crop circle messages?

Yang 2 April 2016 07:14:42

Many crop circles have been decoded, among the most prominent are the Arecibo crop circle and Crabwood.

Name Withheld 2 April 2016 09:28:29

Interesting! I'd check these up on the internet

Denis 2 April 2016 09:34:26

Just enjoy those crazy brain questions = 32, 5, 5, 10, 7. The handbook is now a book.

Crop Circles messages, symbolism :
http://www.ourtransition.info/use Google Translate for some info in Russian

http://www.cropcircleconnector.com/interface2005.htm
and probably here coming soon. Thanks Patrick and TEC.

Chapter 9 - Purposes

Steve 25 March 2016 19:17:38

If they could urgently, but of course, accidentally, bump off orbit, the satellite that transmits, E Channel Network, MTV, Fox News, they would be helping immensely to lift humanity!

Patrick 26 March 2016 15:05:59

Ah, yes … censorship! Our old and good friend …

Mike 27 March 2016 08:11:05

I did read somewhere that the 'tall greys' as it were are the benevolent beings but the 'small greys' as is common in visitations are the least trustworthy. They are the ones abducting and experimenting on humans.

I'd like to invite ET's around to communicate with, but I don't want to be abducted. How can we invite and communicate with them safely?

Would it be in the same way as calling in spirit?

Patrick 29 March 2016 22:04:14

Ask them. They can tune into your thoughts, if they choose to. What response will be received? They might ask you to not tell anyone ... be prepared for that.

Yang 29 March 2016 00:34:42

This (book) ought to be a Discovery/BBC Special or something. The information is so important and profound that it deserves to be known to all mankind.

Throughout the years of reading, I have always wondered why "they" choose text as the medium to channel information and as many others have asked—why not just land on the White House OR the Olympic Arena. Because I believe there is a way to do it progressive rather than "hostile." For example, they could hover over the arena, then send a holographic message that could be recorded by all cameras and the live audience—telling that they are in peace, have always watched over Earth for millions of years, that they are helping and have helped mankind for as long as we have existed. Now comes a time with many changes to Earth but we shouldn't fear but trust our instincts and intuition. We will always be close and help when you need it.

Something like that. It would stir up A LOT in the beginning—yes—but because no official government would ever confess their knowledge, people would still wonder and only 10% would actually believe it.

Well, if ET's are listening to this, you have got a solid advice from an earthling, lol. Bring it on! :)

Mike 29 March 2016 15:50:52

Yang. Am sure someone did a film based on that account. Something around the 4th July lol lol.

Patrick 29 March 2016 22:01:42

Yes, and the reactions—or at least the expectations to react that way—as depicted in that movie, "Independence Day" were not inaccurate. That's the big issue in all this, setting off reactions that do more harm than benefit.

Chapter 10 - What Do They Want Here?

Yang 3 April 2016 13:34:34

I love the last sentence. Thank you Patrick, The Committee and Zebulon.

Mike 3 April 2016 13:56:59

Why weren't the 'gold miners' able to create their own Gold instead of taking ours?

Are there no plans to return any of it?

Patrick 3 April 2016 17:23:08

I thought of that question myself but not until after the session was done. It's answered below in another comment question; the cost to synthesize seems to have been the obstacle. Finding gold elsewhere was much easier. The Committee is telling me, the amounts extracted from Earth and other places, where there were no beings using or taking advantage of it, was vast. Millions of our metric tons I am getting.

Mike 4 April 2016 13:17:23

But surely an interstellar travelling advanced race like these ET's are, they could have easily invented a cost efficient way of mass producing Gold.

Name Withheld 3 April 2016 14:18:35

I was just thinking of asking the same question when I saw that Mike has already asked it. Don't the ETs have technology to synthesize gold? In particle accelerators or nuclear reactors it is already possible to synthesize gold through a process called Nuclear transmutation although the production cost is currently many times the market price of gold. That's why it's not done. Surely the ETs could have invented something to do so cheaply instead of mining it here.

Patrick 3 April 2016 17:39:01

See the answer above to Mike's question.

"Return" the gold? There were no owners of the gold as we understand ownership. In fact we were created by the miners. The concepts of ownership, territory, and control are going to come under interesting review as we learn more about our galactic neighbors.

Yang 3 April 2016 15:18:43

How does the gold "float" in the air?

Patrick 3 April 2016 17:32:04

Any substance will be kept aloft by moving air currents, if it's light enough, and that means small enough particles.

Volcanic ash is stone, it stays in the atmosphere for years.

The Committee is saying the fine to nearly invisible gold dust is easily gathered from the atmosphere as it begins to descend from high altitudes, and is returned.

The explanation they're giving me is the gold is no longer effective if it descends low enough and is difficult to gather and redistribute if allowed to reach the surface. ET technology makes its gathering easy, by sweeping the atmosphere at specific altitudes on a continuous basis.

Yang 4 April 2016 01:21:32

Obviously :) Thank you Patrick!

Steve 3 April 2016 18:55:49

Something inside me just thought, how do you know you are only told the truth by these ETs? Do you rely on the committee for that?

Patrick 3 April 2016 19:54:08

Put another way, how do I know the ETs are not deceiving me? Incentive ... just as this works with humans. Where there is an advantage to be gained by deceiving, some liars make good on that label. They have none. ETs are not asking me for anything. Yes, The Committee would help me, they have alerted me to deceit all my life, and for many years I didn't quite understand the alarm being sounded. I simply thought I had good intuition into peddlers of twisted truth. I've never been warned by The Committee that either an ET or any other entity was not being truthful with me.

Mike 4 April 2016 13:13:19

I know you have told me in the past that your trust and faith in the Committee has been proven. But do you still not every now and then, just for curiosity throw the Committee a curve ball? Just to keep things fresh and focused. I always think it's good to have a critic. It keeps you focused and on the ball.

Chapter 11 - When Will They Come?

Yang 10 April 2016 17:00:02

And really, why should "they" solve "our" problems? WE created them. WE "condone" violence. WE manufacture the weapons before solving world poverty, and then ask for alien intervention to solve it? Weird.

Steve 10 April 2016 18:25:29

I watched a very interesting documentary about The History of Egypt on the weekend, the thing that really stuck with me is the humans in that region have been fighting for thousands of years, and I just can't see how it will ever stop, it's almost like it's in their DNA?

Patrick 10 April 2016 18:54:57

"Their" DNA? It's all ours, my friend.

Janis 18 September 2017 09:56:22

Patrick how many of the readers of the Amendment will experience contact from [alien extraterrestrials] even if the world is not ready? I will be really disappointed if in my lifetime (in my daytime minutes) I don't get the chance. I do enjoy when you interview them.

Patrick 18 September 2017 17:14:46

Very few of us, as in almost none. The Committee is telling me I will be met by some; however I'm not looking forward to becoming known for it. A fair share of humans would quickly come to see me as an ET magnet, then follow me around and even ask me to summon ETs physically. The ETs absolutely would NOT come see me on request, if there were the slightest chance anyone would be around. I'd enjoy meeting them a lot, but how would it improve my life? It wouldn't.

Imagine US Ministry/Dept. of Defense reaction to the perception some Joe Blow (me) can have Arcturans, Pleidians or Sirians over for tea anytime I extend an invitation.

The ETs know this perfectly, so tells me The Committee. The ETs have other plans. As far as a face-to-face meeting, I would welcome it personally but would not discuss it publicly EVER.

The ETs are not going to share technology with humans, not going to solve our "problems" (they can't) or tell us how. At best they might suggest something, but what if anything we do about such suggestions, is up to us. We will solve what we have created or assumed. We can't solve a volcanic eruption or control its effects, but we can live a safe distance away. Aliens aren't going to control nature's events, stop North Korea from launching missiles over Japan, calm down Islamoterrorists, lower taxes, eradicate disease or ... or ... cure the common cold for us.

Most people would reject alien ET suggestions anyway, because they wouldn't like them or would believe I'm a hoax. "How could a human meet & communicate with ETs?" would be the general reaction.

I'm curious about the history of whatever ET civilization might wish to share and demonstrate what it has discovered technologically, but that's it. Even if they told me how propulsion and navigation operate specifically, in order to reach Earth and return home, I'd never discuss it. Why? We can't use it. We made weapons from alien ET technology (atomic bombs) and we'd probably do the same thing with many technologies. (Yes, we reverse engineered an atomic reactor found aboard an alien ET scout ship, but we have NO IDEA how to magnetically suspend a tiny amount of fissile material molecules for use in a small, safe reaction to generate simple heat, electricity thus magnetism.)

We're not prepared to venture into space any more than we can build a submarine to safely descend a crew to a depth of 10 kilometers below the ocean's surface. Such information would serve what purpose? Satisfy curiosity and entertain us, just like a good Star Trek episode, but nothing more.

I understand this sounds strange coming from the author of a book on aliens, but I feel compelled to channel them. I simply do not want to be their ambassador or the representative of the human race, as other humans might see it.

The alien ETs who know of us well and have scheduled plans to reveal their presence, do not need a human representative or ambassador, and if I presented myself as one to mankind, I'd be hounded and hunted like dog by my fellow humans.

So.
Would.
You.

You might think I've already met with them and I'm concealing it. Maybe. Doesn't matter if I did or did not.

Lorri 19 September 2017 04:00:34

I've never been a UFO nut, but I'd still like to see a UFO and I'd like to see an ET. I'd especially like to communicate with one.

However, I never thought it would help me in any way, nor do I think it will ever happen. There is nothing about me that gives them any reason to contact me. I'm not a scientific person who would be looking to exchange any information.

It would only be for the experience.

If they want mankind to get used to their presence, I guess they should keep on allowing videos to be made of their ships, which they are already doing. The more of that material there is to look at, the quicker people will begin to accept it. The videos need to be clearer though.

Patrick 19 September 2017 13:18:29

The videos will be clearer BECAUSE the human who made the video can also be identified and attest to where, how and when. Without that component, it'll all be written off as a hoax.

Gerry 18 September 2017 21:33:56

Hi Patrick and Committee, is it the challenges that the Shift is bringing or is it the wide spread knowledge /disclosure of aliens that will be bringing humanity closer together? Or do such things just change our day to day priorities as we continue to see ourselves and countries/cultures as different and separate from one another?

Thanks

Patrick 19 September 2017 13:13:20

The Shift is what's doing it and will continue. Alien ETs will simply be advisors and counselors, hopefully we listen well. Bring humanity closer together?

For now, that mostly means "agree with me."

Coming closer together = giving in somewhat.

We humans have a very poor track record on that. As soon as one side of an issue believes it has extracted a concession from the "opposition," does it say thank you, then stand down and counsel everyone how good that was OR do the planning, scheming and machinations continue, in order to extract more concessions while giving in as little as possible? In other words, what most politicians do reflexively?

OK, let's toss all politicians.

Will we create new ones?
We always have, no matter what.

Who wants to erase pieces of their culture or be told how ingrained habits are not helpful? I've never met that person.

Example: the President of the USA, in frustration with "his" party (not really, half of them can't stand Trump's guts) approached the political opposition's leadership to suggest a compromise arrangement on taxes and illegal alien children (I'm not sure). The reaction from both sides was negative; "watch out, don't trust him" from the other party and from the President's own? A traitor! A turncoat!

We cannot compromise very well. We're going to learn in ways we have not done in MANY millennia.

Stephen 18 September 2017 23:16:36

Patrick is not the first or last person to communicate with ET's.

Other people who have such experience are not hounded by the public, and so, no need to worry too much.

I consider communication with ET's and channeling messages from other dimensions all part of an effort to inform and prepare the public for the Shift and 'official and public' arrival of ET's.

So that when the Shift becomes apparent or un-deniable, or when ET lands at the White House lawn, enough of the public is already prepared for such eventuality.

If ET is not going to annihilate humanity or bestow any new technology upon humanity, is there any practical purpose for such communication, other than curiosity satisfaction?

(Let's ignore alien abduction for now.) Of course there is. because the truth is of utmost importance. When Copernicus expounded on the fact that Earth rotates around the sun, and not vice versa, it was of little practical importance then. I would say the practical use of such knowledge has increased exponentially since then.

Until a flying saucer lands on the White House lawn, there are always people denouncing the existence of ET and spirits. But never mind. I believe the number of open-minded people willing to open their eyes and see the truth increasing everyday. All thanks to the effort of Patrick and other volunteers who provide us with invaluable channeled information.

Patrick 19 September 2017 12:54:06

Communicate is one thing, meet with them another. We're not hounded because nobody believes there are alien ETs to see, meet, touch, etc. The very millisecond belief spreads that physical meetings with alien ETs have happened and could again, the press blood hounds will be barking and running. The practical purpose is to make mankind aware of our origins and place in the galaxy. This will open the door to greater awareness, understanding and growth of our souls. We'll see alternatives to the violence and war we haven't overcome, which we continue to propagate. Exhibit A - North Korea at the moment.

Why carry a protective sidearm, say in the case of law enforcement? 99% of humanity would never physically threaten or harm a cop (or anyone else). BUT that's the problem, we're stuck on 99%. Despite the finest efforts of institutions such as law enforcement, courts, jails, drug rehabilitation, psychologists, psychiatrists, medical doctors, counselors, families, friends and the list goes on … we're stuck on 99%. Nobody has figured out how to make 99.999% calm down and stop harming one another.

How nice to live in a society where you truly do not have to worry about assault, theft, rape, robbery, burglary, terrorism or murder EVER? How do we achieve this? Alien ETs will show us, and we will have the opportunity to change course. Alien ET gadgets are beside the point, and they know it.

Linda H 19 September 2017 01:40:23

1)   Are the AEs like the one communicated with in this post of a 3D or 4D vibration?
2)   Is this the same as those scheduled to make "first" contact?
3)   Do you know if the ET communicated with in the post was one of the ETs represented in the picture?

Patrick 19 September 2017 12:38:57

1.   High fourth and occasionally, briefly, fifth dimension.
2.   No, and there is no first contact to be made, which already happened millions of Earth years ago. Contacts are made all the time.
    You refer to contact widely recognized, acknowledged and accepted? Every raging inferno started out the size of a match before it grew to a large fire then conflagration.
3.   Humans would definitely recognize a conflagration of alien ET ships landing and we'd also recognize the military response, a virtual

certainty in such instance. Even if no shots were fired by us (useless anyway) and the encounter became a Mexican standoff, where would this have to take place for press, video and reporters to record it to such point the general public believes it? Such required location guarantees a security response, the last thing our ET cousins want to set off.

Chapter 12 - The Future of ETs with Earth

Yang 11 April 2016 01:17:24

Thank you the Committee and Patrick for a well written chapter—It is with excitement and wonder I will look into the glimpses of the future you are providing us with.

One could think that our integration into the galactic community should be the number one topic on the human agenda, instead we argue which presidential candidate has the biggest "d**k." So no wonder we are not yet prepared for a disclosure of ET species!

Again, thank you both.

Steve 11 April 2016 02:36:57

Yes, Yang, how true, but, by the way, my guess would be Hillary.

Yang 11 April 2016 06:55:22

From a galactic perspective, maybe Donald is more open to ET-disclosure. We know for a fact that Hillary has the same agenda as previous Clintons and "Bushes" and they won't say much, so there we have maybe another indicator that at least a republican will be the winner (if there is such thing) IF ET disclosure is a near-future probability.

Lorri 11 April 2016 08:15:08

I would think ending war, world hunger, and other human tragedies would be the number one topic on the human agenda, especially when you consider that the galactic community is largely a mystery to humans.

Yang 11 April 2016 10:14:04

Yes, one could argue that too. It is not wrong, but this is my reasoning:

1. The ET agenda is an allowance from the people that secrecy, information manipulation, enclosure of facts and elite-driven democracy is accepted
2. If we remove this "veil", we take the first step for an open information society, where government representatives take a higher personal responsibility to inform the PEOPLE not protecting the very organisation they represent
3. When open information is generally accepted, BANK and MONEY can't rule the same any more. There must be a different system to supersede the old interest- and helicopter money based system that a few people have constructed not for the benefit of the larger mass.
4. Poverty, hunger, war is now easier to solve because they in fact represent the values of secrecy, information enclosure and greed that the current system is based on.

Because GREED, MONEY, ELITISM feed on secrecy and enclosures and my belief is that these are the sole reasons why we have war, hunger and injustices in the first place.

Patrick 12 April 2016 11:24:58

Everything described here is a human creation. We collectively continue all these things some—many of us—say we dislike. Solutions are NOT coming from extraterrestrial visitors.

Name Withheld 11 April 2016 10:11:55

1. It appears from me that aliens are somehow pro-actively involved in not letting nuclear war happen rather than leaving it to human free will. Is it a correct observation? Were the aliens somehow involved in stopping nuclear weapon testing and preventing nuclear war?
2. Apart from the harm that a nuclear explosion does to the earth (e.g. radiation), how does it cause effects in realms beyond earth and what kind of effects? Can you explain it in a little bit more detail and the realms which it affects and how?
3. On earth, apparently Chernobyl and Fukushima nuclear plant disasters were more devastating in the long term than, say, nuclear weapons used in Hiroshima and Nagasaki. While more people died in Hiroshima and Nagasaki, people at least stay in those cities now. But nobody stays at Fukushima or Chernobyl. So, how can nuclear weapons cause disturbance in other realms while nuclear plants do not, although essentially both use the same processes?

Patrick 12 April 2016 12:04:29

1.   Yes; both ETs and our GAGs are directly, not just somehow involved.

2.   Human death, suffering and injury are felt by our guides just as we might feel them, and often more. Mass deaths and genocide are felt in a logarithmically higher proportion; a human example is from the Star Wars movies, "a disturbance in the force." Two people dead are not double the effect of one death, and four people killed are not double the effect of two deaths. As the number of dead increase, the effect multiplies in greater proportions than the numbers suggest.

When nuclear weapons have killed many thousands and thousands on Earth, the effects reverberate across the galaxy in a dreadful, horrible way. Unwanted, large group departures of souls from their bodies are seen and felt the same way humans would, if forced to watch human limbs ripped from living victims.

3.   Nuclear weapons deplete nearly all the fissile material in less than a second. This mass, sudden release of energy—an explosion—creates intense light, heat, and radiation. The effects of radioactive fallout linger but dissipate to safe levels within time.

The nuclear cores of power plants are intentionally closed in, not designed to explode. They leak—spew is a better word—dangerous levels of radiation for long stretches. Human approach to attempt to stop the reaction is suicidal exposure to radiation.

To answer both questions about disturbances in other realms; what happens is the effect of mass deaths. Murder, to our guardian angel guides, is just as, IF NOT MORE, horrific than it is to humans.

The effects of a great, mass crying out send shock waves of grief through the galaxy and even into other galaxies. No good purpose is served.

We humans who comprise mankind have discovered how to "play with matches" of the nuclear variety and burn down entire stadiums, killing thousands unable to escape. Beyond the immediately dead, what about friends and families? The severely injured who linger in great distress and suffer horribly before dying. Detonations of nuclear weapons create this effect throughout the galaxy, to the billions of spirits and souls who are our true families. Unlike individual circumstances of unexpected death, where individual meaning and purpose can be served (we all die eventually) NO good comes from mass slaughter of humans at the hands of humans. We have discovered and misused this ability, with expected effects. Because of it, we are not to be allowed more mass slaughter by the tens of thousands and millions.

Nearly all humans incarnated on Earth since 1945 have written this into their life contracts.

believer 12 April 2016 17:39:53

This feels like a contradiction. We have free will. There is a huge post about how our cousins would never interfere with humanity and our choices, except for this technology in weapon form.

On this post on another human weapon that has taken many more lives than the use of nuclear explosives have, free will of humans is invoked and the point is made that anything literally can be made into a weapon to kill another life. So which is it? Are we free or aren't we? Humans have the right to burn ourselves with matches to learn or not?

If the explanation that the effects on other beings in different dimensions that we do not get that we are hurting is to be believed, then why were the first two uses of the weapon allowed? Why didn't they stop the two weapons from working like they do now?

If I recall correctly, a previous explanation was that the WW2 weapons were allowed to go off to teach us/allow humanity to learn through experience how dangerous nukes were, with the further explanation that because they were relatively weak, they also weren't damaging. By that logic, shouldn't suitcase nukes or North Korea's low technology/low enriched weapons be allowed to go off?

Seems we are living under imposed weapon control laws imposed by our cousins, and it just doesn't seem to mesh with the messages of interference with free will. If these weapons do indeed rip apart the environment and/or being of other dimensions shouldn't our use of these weapons (and possession I guess) prompt a formal intervention by our cousins to the everyman and not just global leader elites so that humanity is more aware of this issue and not left ignorant while our "leaders" which we put there in our ignorance, since we don't fully comprehend nukes, knows via our cousins but because of corruption/power keeps them in our world for advantage over other nation states? Doesn't informing the populace make more sense than seemingly failing to convince the powerful leaders to get rid of them if this is indeed important?

Since weapons is the issue I will also mention the repeated messaging about our cousins in regards to mass shootings involving guns seems to be o.k. explained by contracts.

So why aren't there interdimensional contracts like the human deaths in ww2 have? Why are our cousins drawing a line? We have free will or we do not. Our cousins either allow humanity their free will or they don't. And they don't. So all the free will arguments about Columbine seem to fall flat when there is a given set of facts where our free will is interfered with without communication to us at the individual level.

That sounds more like rats being manipulated in a cage without their ability to see the strings being pulled outside that cage.

So do we have free will, or don't we?

If human lives are expendable because they are just flesh bodies, why are other beings in other dimensions any different that they need to be protected from us and why are nukes some breaking point where this doesn't apply?

I can't get past this seeming contradiction.

Patrick 12 April 2016 18:39:08

"So which is it?"
BOTH.

In theory we could annihilate ourselves with poisons, pollution, plagues, disease, epidemics, (non-nuclear) wars ... these things would proceed at a steady pace. Maybe rapidly, maybe slowly but if mankind chose to do this, it would affect only mankind.

As soon as humans do something that interferes with existence and civilizations from & on other planets, we are intervening WITH THEM. Aside from nuclear weapons, we do not have the ability to annihilate all life on Earth in one quick conflagration OR to disturb "The Force". Long before conventional bombing could end most Earth life, there would be so few humans left to continue the attacks to kill off all life, that many plants, insects, birds, snakes, etc etc would survive. Many humans likely would also.

Humans now have the nuclear capability to kill off almost all life on Earth and if we did so, the combinations of energy, sub-atomic particles released and mass soul returns to Heaven would disturb THEM horribly.

This is very different from two nations, a band of terrorists and victims of starvation in the immediate area. There are well more than 100 million births per year on Earth, >250 per minute. More than forty percent of this amount also die, each year.

In a nuclear exchange, the number of annual births x 3 or 4 would die in one or two hours. Billions of us would perish in a matter of weeks. Such a scenario would reach FAR beyond free will. Humanity is not as isolated from our galaxial community as we think we are (and frankly, most humans would consider belief in a galaxial community to be a mental disorder), and because there is no accepted scientific evidence to "prove" it yet (we don't understand this science) it is challenging to imagine what we could do as threatening well-being away from Earth.

We humans say "well-being" and we instinctively think "body" before we consider minds. Where there are no dense Earth bodies in a dimensionally limited environment like Earth, body and soul are the same; there is either no body or one much "lighter" and more connected to its energetic essence.

The first two uses were allowed because those weapons were firecrackers by comparison to today's warheads. By the 1960s nuclear weapons were 3,000 times as powerful. Imagine today and how many more there are?

Lorri 12 April 2016 17:58:40

I was also wondering about what believer brought up.

If everything is left up to us to fix, then why are nuclear weapons different? Also, I am confused by the message that ETs and guides feel even worse than we do at seeing human tragedy. When I asked how they felt a few days ago about seeing children starve because of war, they said they didn't react.

I am utterly confused now.

Patrick 12 April 2016 18:49:47

"If everything is left up to us to fix" ... Fix is a VERY subjective term. We humans have the opportunity to change what we create. We don't attempt to "fix" tornadoes, we know we don't cause them; we avoid them, or try. Starvation because of war? We start the wars. Starvation? We've proven we can produce (and waste a lot of) food. MASS human deaths that affect them. They don't emotionally react to what humans do that is independent of them; they simply observe. As soon as humans do something that might hurt THEM, they prevent.

Denis 12 April 2016 09:14:47

Patrick, a great handbook, hope you can convince one of the publisher to market the book.

Now we wait for these guys to show up and land when we have raised our vibrations worldwide which will tell them it is ok to do so.

Patrick 12 April 2016 12:13:33

The vast majority of humans will only hear about ET contacts in the news—those even hearing any news—and half of them will not believe what's reported. Most of the others will eventually forget, when it becomes obvious ETs are not taking over, interceding or -fering in human societies. A good deal of time, maybe a decade or two, will have to pass before more regular contact of a diplomatic nature takes its course. Humanity will come to expect that ETs are not going to interfere with Earth any more than we can interfere with their home planets. We can't even determine there are ET planets, much less go to them. ET contact with mankind is going to be subtle, gentle, and minimal. That won't sell many tickets, so we'll all move onto the next Zika virus scare, political scandal, economic crisis, and world cup.

About the Author

I am a baby boomer born in Queens, New York USA to an immigrant father and granddaughter-of-immigrants mother, raised in its suburbs, the middle son of three.

We got married in 1986 and still are; we have 2 grown children, one married with a grandchild on the way.

An exchange student in Mexico as a teenager, I worked for three decades in commercial insurance, living along the way in Saudi Arabia, Brazil and Colombia. I've visited dozens of countries, many for work and also two thirds of the United States. I moved to Texas, where I still and always intended to live, nineteen years before this book's publication.

I am multilingual.

My channeling & writing began in 2012.

My website: www.theamendment.net

There are eight popular, regularly selling e-books on Amazon.com, the archives of channeling sessions from 2012-17. To maintain a handy size & length, new editions become available approximately twice per year.

Other Books by Ozark Mountain Publishing, Inc.

Dolores Cannon
A Soul Remembers Hiroshima
Between Death and Life
Conversations with Nostradamus,
    Volume I, II, III
The Convoluted Universe -Book One,
    Two, Three, Four, Five
The Custodians
Five Lives Remembered
Jesus and the Essenes
Keepers of the Garden
Legacy from the Stars
The Legend of Starcrash
The Search for Hidden Sacred Knowledge
They Walked with Jesus
The Three Waves of Volunteers and the
    New Earth
Aron Abrahamsen
Holiday in Heaven
Out of the Archives – Earth Changes
Justine Alessi & M. E. McMillan
Rebirth of the Oracle
Kathryn/Patrick Andries
Naked in Public
Kathryn Andries
The Big Desire
Dream Doctor
Soul Choices: Six Paths to Find Your Life
    Purpose
Soul Choices: Six Paths to Fulfilling
    Relationships
Patrick Andries
Owners Manual for the Mind
Tom Arbino
You Were Destined to be Together
Rev. Keith Bender
The Despiritualized Church
Dan Bird
Waking Up in the Spiritual Age
O.T. Bonnett, M.D./Greg Satre
Reincarnation: The View from Eternity
What I Learned After Medical School
Why Healing Happens
Julia Cannon
Soul Speak – The Language of Your Body
Ronald Chapman
Seeing True
Albert Cheung
The Emperor's Stargate
Jack Churchward
Lifting the Veil on the Lost Continent of
    Mu
The Stone Tablets of Mu
Sherri Cortland
Guide Group Fridays
Raising Our Vibrations for the New Age

Spiritual Tool Box
Windows of Opportunity
Cinnamon Crow
Chakra Zodiac Healing Oracle
Teen Oracle
Patrick De Haan
The Alien Handbook
Michael Dennis
Morning Coffee with God
God's Many Mansions
Claire Doyle Beland
Luck Doesn't Happen by Chance
Jodi Felice
The Enchanted Garden
Max Flindt/Otto Binder
Mankind: Children of the Stars
Arun & Sunanda Gandhi
The Forgotten Woman
Maiya & Geoff Gray-Cobb
Angels -The Guardians of Your Destiny
Seeds of the Soul
Carolyn Greer Daly
Opening to Fullness of Spirit
Julia Hanson
Awakening to Your Creation
Donald L. Hicks
The Divinity Factor
Anita Holmes
Twidders
Antoinette Lee Howard
Journey Through Fear
Vara Humphreys
The Science of Knowledge
Victoria Hunt
Kiss the Wind
James H. Kent
Past Life Memories as A Confederate
    Soldier
Mandeep Khera
Why?
Dorothy Leon
Is Jehovah an E.T
Mary Letorney
Discover the Universe Within You
Diane Lewis
From Psychic to Soul
Sture Lönnerstrand
I Have Lived Before
Donna Lynn
From Fear to Love
Irene Lucas
Thirty Miracles in Thirty Days
Susan Mack & Natalia Krawetz
My Teachers Wear Fur Coats
Patrick McNamara
Beauty and the Priest

Other Books by Ozark Mountain Publishing, Inc.

Maureen McGill
Baby It's You
Maureen McGill & Nola Davis
Live from the Other Side
Henry Michaelson
And Jesus Said – A Conversation
Dennis Milner
Kosmos
Andy Myers
Not Your Average Angel Book
Guy Needler
Avoiding Karma
Beyond the Source – Book 1, Book 2
The Anne Dialogues
The History of God
The Origin Speaks
James Nussbaumer
And Then I Knew My Abundance
The Master of Everything
Mastering Your Own Spiritual Freedom
Sherry O'Brian
Peaks and Valleys
Riet Okken
The Liberating Power of Emotions
John Panella
The Gnostic Papers
Victor Parachin
Sit a Bit
Nikki Pattillo
A Spiritual Evolution
Children of the Stars
Rev. Grant H. Pealer
A Funny Thing Happened on the
    Way to Heaven
Worlds Beyond Death
Karen Peebles
The Other Side of Suicide
Victoria Pendragon
Born Healers
Feng Shui from the Inside, Out
Sleep Magic
The Sleeping Phoenix
Michael Perlin
Fantastic Adventures in Metaphysics
Walter Pullen
Evolution of the Spirit
Christine Ramos, RN
A Journey into Being
Debra Rayburn
Let's Get Natural with Herbs
Charmian Redwood
A New Earth Rising
Coming Home to Lemuria

David Rivinus
Always Dreaming
Briceida Ryan
The Ultimate Dictionary of Dream
    Language
M. Don Schorn
Elder Gods of Antiquity
Legacy of the Elder Gods
Gardens of the Elder Gods
Reincarnation...Stepping Stones of Life
Garnet Schulhauser
Dance of Eternal Rapture
Dance of Heavenly Bliss
Dancing Forever with Spirit
Dancing on a Stamp
Annie Stillwater Gray
Education of a Guardian Angel
The Dawn Book
Work of a Guardian Angel
Blair Styra
Don't Change the Channel
Natalie Sudman
Application of Impossible Things
L.R. Sumpter
We Are the Creators
Dee Wallace/Jarrad Hewett
The Big E
Dee Wallace
Conscious Creation
James Wawro
Ask Your Inner Voice
Janie Wells
Embracing the Human Journey
Payment for Passage
Dennis Wheatley/ Maria Wheatley
The Essential Dowsing Guide
Maria Wheatley
Druidic Soul Star Astrology
Jacquelyn Wiersma
The Zodiac Recipe
Sherry Wilde
The Forgotten Promise
Lyn Willmoth
A Small Book of Comfort
Stuart Wilson & Joanna Prentis
Atlantis and the New Consciousness
Beyond Limitations
The Essenes -Children of the Light
The Magdalene Version
Power of the Magdalene
Robert Winterhalter
The Healing Christ

For more information about any of the above titles, soon to be released titles,
or other items in our catalog, write, phone or visit our website:
PO Box 754, Huntsville, AR 72740
479-738-2348/800-935-0045
www.ozarkmt.com